SAGE Guide to
Social Work Careers

SAGE Guide to Social Work Careers

Your Journey to Advocacy

Melissa Bird
Portland State University

Los Angeles | London | New Delhi
Singapore | Washington DC | Melbourne

FOR INFORMATION:

SAGE Publications, Inc.
2455 Teller Road
Thousand Oaks, California 91320
E-mail: order@sagepub.com

SAGE Publications Ltd.
1 Oliver's Yard
55 City Road
London EC1Y 1SP
United Kingdom

SAGE Publications India Pvt. Ltd.
B 1/I 1 Mohan Cooperative Industrial Area
Mathura Road, New Delhi 110 044
India

SAGE Publications Asia-Pacific Pte. Ltd.
3 Church Street
#10–04 Samsung Hub
Singapore 049483

Printed in the United States of America

ISBN: 978-1-5443-2471-5

This book is printed on acid-free paper.

Acquisitions Editor: Joshua Perigo
Editorial Assistant: Alexandra Randall
Production Editor: Jane Martinez
Copy Editor: Colleen Brennan
Typesetter: C&M Digitals (P) Ltd.
Proofreader: Alison Syring
Cover Designer: Candice Harman
Marketing Manager: Katherine Hepburn

18 19 20 21 22 10 9 8 7 6 5 4 3 2 1

CONTENTS

PREFACE

In 2001 I entered my master of social work (MSW) program with every intent of becoming a play therapist. In my mind, what better way could there be to help kids and at the same time get paid to play all day? We began our program in August. One month later the 9/11 terrorist attacks on New York and Washington, D.C., happened, and all of the things that we thought we knew for sure were destroyed. What happened after that day changed the entire trajectory of my career as a social worker. Our professors shifted our entire policy curriculum to learning about the Middle East and policies that affect immigration, and they became committed to creating well-trained advocates out of each of us. The next year I took the mandatory policy class from Dr. Emma Gross, and the way she taught us about policy and advocacy got me hooked and I was never the same again.

Every person in the social work profession has the ability to make deep impacts on the communities in which they work. Because of our allegiance to social justice, we are the individuals in America whose passions will contribute to great change in individual lives. Each one of us has a unique talent and perspective to offer to the world of social welfare. What we choose to do with that talent can take many forms, including that of social justice advocacy. As a member of the lesbian, gay, bisexual, and transgender (LGBT) community, I knew that LGBT homeless youth were at great risk for experiencing multiple traumas and discrimination. It was my passion for my community that started me down the road to social justice advocacy. Many times I had to create my own jobs at nonprofit organizations so that I could engage in social justice work. Sometimes I didn't get paid what I was worth, but at every turn I was successful because my education as a social worker gave me the foundation to build coalitions and improve systems.

This book came about because the publisher and I recognized that although the social work profession has done a phenomenal job providing guidance to bachelor of social work (BSW) and MSW students about opportunities to engage in social welfare professions in clinical practice, there is little literature offering guidance for social work students whose dreams and aspirations are leading them toward a career in social justice and advocacy work.

Each of us enters the social work profession with a commitment to serve others. For some of us that means that we pursue a career with youth, for others the elderly, for still others we have a deep sense that if we engage in change on a community level, our career aspirations will be met as we work to directly impact systems of care. All social workers are born advocates; we just need the tools to build a robust career in policy and advocacy work. This book is part of that toolbox.

This book offers you a strategy that can be used to effect broad policy change in all political climates. It draws on fundamentals of the social work profession, such as coalition building, advocacy engagement, and stakeholder outreach. This book provides a blueprint for social workers to become engaged in the political arena to pass legislation and engage in micro-, mezzo-, and macro-level advocacy efforts that can lead to policy change. It is my hope that this book will be used by social workers and social workers in training to deepen their commitment to social justice advocacy and facilitate their engagement in making policy change.

The difference between this book and other career books is the singular focus on social justice and advocacy work. Many social work career books focus on clinical work, sometimes devoting only one chapter to careers in advocacy and social justice. This book is different in that it is infused with the passions of social workers around the country who have engaged in advocacy change, and it gives the reader real-time examples of career opportunities around the country that can lead to a robust career in social justice advocacy.

Given the current state of politics in the United States and the policy attacks on the safety net and social welfare structure, a book that can give students the information they need to make informed decisions about their careers, especially in advocacy and social justice, is timely and necessary. This is that book.

The second year of my MSW program I called Dr. Emma Gross on the phone. I was waiting for my 5 p.m. class to start and standing in front of the vending machine wondering which dinner snacks I was going to have because I had forgotten to pack a meal. I asked her how I could get a job doing advocacy in Salt Lake City in the LGBT community. She assured me that I would have to move somewhere else, perhaps Los Angeles or New York City.

Flash forward 15 years later and I have been teaching macro social work and policy and advocacy classes for over 5 years at multiple public and private universities. I have been practicing in the field of macro social work since obtaining my master's degree in 2003 and have written six pieces of legislation that have been passed by the Utah State Legislature. I have personal and professional advocacy experience from the community level through the federal level. I obtained my PhD in social work and a gender studies certificate from the University of Southern California in 2017. As an expert in the field of social welfare policy and advocacy, I have published numerous articles to inform and train future generations of social workers to engage in advocacy efforts.

I was once told I would never have a successful career in social welfare advocacy. I am proof that sometimes when it comes to getting advice about a career in advocacy, social work educators get it wrong. That is why I wrote this book. Each chapter details how social workers can pursue a career in social justice based on the subject of the chapter. In each chapter, advocates from around the country have provided their personal stories, highlighting their successes in advocacy practice. I hope that as you read the stories and job descriptions, you will begin to see yourself in one or two of these areas of practice and you will recognize your potential for greatness as you pursue a career that doesn't just change the life of one person but the lives of many people.

Throughout the book, you are not just given the opportunity to learn how to follow a path to social work advocacy but you will be encouraged to tap into what you are passionate about so you can successfully navigate the field of advocacy as a career. Welcome to your journey. Please let me know how it goes.

ACKNOWLEDGMENTS

This book would not be possible without the help of some of the most remarkable social justice workers in the nation. Sonya Martinez, Beth Davenport, Kathryn Rehner, Dr. Kristie Holmes, Dr. Angela Henderson, Tasha Perdue Forquer, Dr. Troy Christian Anderson, Dr. Gretchen Heidemann Whitt, and Maryann Martindale. These colleagues and friends are a continual inspiration to me and I am so appreciative they are in my life. To Nicole Aston for her assistance and research: You are one of the most inquisitive students I have ever taught, and I am proud beyond measure to be your mentor. To my husband, James Thomas Kelly, and my three children, Katelynn, Gwendelynn, and Sean, I am eternally grateful that you chose me to be yours. To the hundreds of students I have taught over the years, this book has come about because of all of you; thank you for being *my* greatest teacher.

ABOUT THE AUTHOR

Nathalie Gordon
http://www.nathaliegordon.com/

Melissa Bird, PhD, MSW, is a passionate feminist whose education in social work has led to a career advocating for children, women, and their families. She is a fierce believer in social justice advocacy and preparing women for leadership roles in politics. She has a wealth of experience working with policy makers, community leaders, and other stakeholders to improve access to reproductive health care for women, men, and teens.

As a writer, professor, and fiery public speaker, Dr. Bird creates the genesis for a new brand of leadership. Her words awaken revolutionaries, trailblazers, and powerful innovators in the quest for justice. When she's not building her public speaking empire, she can be found reading trashy novels, drinking fine whiskey, playing mom to three delicious humans, and loving her punk rock scientist James Thomas Kelly.

Connect with Missy at birdgirlindustries.com and on Facebook, Twitter, and Instagram @birdgirl1001.

FOLLOW YOUR PASSION, NOT JUST A PATH

I remember the first time I advocated for something. I was a 17-year-old senior in high school and I was fired up about this new word I had learned, a word that was uttered with this guttural undertone that was at once full of awe and rage. When people said it, they had a visceral reaction to it—it either turned them on or turned them off. I wanted to completely immerse myself in it. I wanted to become it. I wanted to infuse its power into the very fibers of my being until I literally glowed with the essence of all of its glorious meaning. I wanted that word taught to every single student in my high school because I figured that if everyone knew and understood the word, then maybe the harassment and groping of girls would stop. Maybe my gay friend wouldn't be bullied anymore. Maybe I would have the strength to tell an adult that I was grieving the suicide of my father 10 years earlier and not be seen as weak.

The word is *feminist*. And what it meant to me then is entirely different than what it means to me now, but the foundational pull of feminism has never wavered for me. You see, the slab of concrete on which feminism is situated is composed of justice, advocacy, fairness, and equality. These things mix together to become the blend of fuel that drives my passion and fills my soul with a fire that cannot be extinguished. It is feminism that has created endless possibility for social change throughout my life, and it is feminism that has allowed me to create a world for social workers to become social justice advocates by following their passion instead of a prescribed path.

All of us have a passion that we can tap into. For me it is feminism; for you it might be something else. What is it that made you consider a degree in social work in the first place? Did you want to work with children or the elderly? Did you have an experience with someone who experienced substance abuse? Perhaps you or someone in your family has a disability? You are going to hear a lot of assumptions about what it means to work in the social work profession. Many of my students believe they won't make any money. I want you to put the negative things you hear about social work aside and know that you *can* make change and move the needle, whether it be for one person or an entire system. Whatever it is that drove you to social work, I hope that this book inspires you to take your social work career one step further as you consider the changes you can make on a local and even a national scale.

I am a teacher. I am a social worker. I am a revolutionary and a change agent. I believe that creative thinking inspires ideas that inspire change. I believe in a new brand of advocacy where we humble ourselves to our shortcomings and engage in acts of Graceful Revolution that bring light to the true reality of people's lives. I believe that if social workers engage people in their own spaces, teach them to look at injustices as moments that touch all of us, if we give them the knowledge of the power structure and the tools to infiltrate its membrane, then change will take place in America. This is the Graceful Revolution and it is the revolution that social workers MUST engage in if we are to protect the safety net and ensure that we are living by the National Association of Social Workers (NASW) Code of Ethics, by which we are bound.

This code of ethical standards is deeply relevant to the professional activities of all social workers, and I believe it is even more so for those who choose to pursue careers in social justice and advocacy. These standards concern social workers' ethical responsibilities to clients, to colleagues, in practice settings, as professionals, to the social work profession, and to the broader society (NASW, 2017).

As social workers, we "have an ethical obligation to engage in actions that bring our clients closer to fairness, justice, and equality" (Bird, 2016, p. 259). Because our profession was erected on these foundational imperatives, it is up to many of us to commit to fully expressing our ethical obligation by pursuing careers in the advocacy field. For some of you, this feels like a dramatic leap; for others, you may already know that you would love nothing more than to influence policy change at a local and national level. For those of you in the middle, know that you aren't alone.

Social workers are uniquely suited to pursue social justice advocacy as a career. We are trained to approach people where they are, not where we want them to be. We are trained in a wide variety of political and social welfare problems that we can directly impact by establishing relationships with people in power. We are trained to find common ground by collectively working together in collaboration with communities and organizations. It is the deep understanding within each one of us that knowing someone's background and story is key to deepening personal relationships in order to influence change in others. It is this notion that is one of the fundamental drivers for engaging with people in power. By developing deep and meaningful relationships, we can advance social justice agendas that are in keeping with our ethical promise to communities and our clients.

Thoughtful dialogue, coalition building, the negotiation of conflict, and thoughtful conversation in the face of adversity are the tools that build a career in social justice advocacy. These tools can be used to shift the way a hospital addresses the needs of a terminally ill patient, the way an organization fights for racial justice in a community, and the way a lobbyist works to achieve policy goals. Careers in social justice advocacy are built on straightforward social justice messages that are effective as long as you are clear about your passion and purpose.

"Our passion for equality and justice is bolstered by the companionship of others who are willing to do what it takes to help others rise" (Bird, 2016, p. 260). As professional social workers, we have firsthand knowledge of the lived experiences of vulnerable people. We are able to communicate the stories of others in a way that influences policy makers and stakeholders to make policy choices that can positively or negatively impact all of our communities for years to come. Working within our communities, we are able to bring together powerful people to ensure that social and economic climates offer opportunities for people to prosper in their lives, to safeguard the elderly from social isolation and poor medical outcomes, to make certain that the lives of transgender women of color do not meet with the violent end that has become so common in America. Embracing a career in social justice advocacy is about embracing the passion within yourself while building relationships with others so that others can more fully understand your position, thus making them more willing to work with you so that you can make lasting, meaningful policy change.

This book is structured to give you inspiration to follow your passion by providing real-life examples of social workers all over the country who in one way or another have engaged in social justice advocacy at a micro, mezzo, or macro level. Each of our contributors has a story of how their social work training led them directly into successful social justice advocacy careers. I have also researched potential career trajectories for each of the chapters so that you can think creatively about pursuing an advocacy career in mental health, disability, or any of the other topics that we cover. Some of these jobs are entry-level positions, some are high-level positions, and some are in between. They are presented here to give you a scope of opportunity and give structure to your arguments about why you are pursuing a career in social justice work. Finally, I provide you with policy examples so that you can actively piece together a full picture of your advocacy career.

It is my hope that by embracing this social justice agenda, you will be able to deeply affect the lives of everyone in your community by pursuing your passion for social justice on behalf of all of the people we serve.

One of the critical components to becoming successful in a career in social justice advocacy is answering these two questions: What is your mission in the world? What lights you on fire? If you cannot answer these questions, then you will be much more likely to have a career that derails than a career that completely stimulates and encourages you while providing you with an income that supports your life.

The fact that I am able to write this book and you are able to read it is a revolutionary act within itself. History tells us that not so long ago, a group of women meeting together in public was scandalous. People of color were specifically banned from congregating in groups, for fear of rebellion. For our entire history, the marginalized were arrested, beaten, and force-fed, but many continued to fight because they knew that if they were able to build community, they would have a voice. As of this writing we are at a tipping point as a nation. Racists have taken to the streets in Charlottesville and we have experienced yet another mass shooting, this time in Las Vegas. Women have been banned from using birth control, and Deferred Action for Childhood Arrivals (DACA) recipients are now living in fear of deportation.

Now is not the time to follow the easy path in our career choices; now is the time to tap into what makes us feel passionate so that we can be the ones to tip the nation in a new direction. As social workers, we are uniquely positioned to engage in social justice advocacy because we are trained to do so throughout our educational experiences. Tuning into your passion is simple. Think of a time when you were afraid of being imperfect and vulnerable. How did that feeling stop you from making a change in your life? Who did you reach out to in order to rise above that fear? The idea of being imperfect and vulnerable stops us from finding commonalities with others. It stops us from engaging in advocacy because we are worried of doing it wrong. The greatest thing about advocacy is there is no wrong way to do it if you are steadfast and committed to your goal. If you know your mission and are tapped into your own personal purpose, engaging in acts of social justice advocacy can be wildly successful. Do not hold back on your passion. It is OK to speak out and be different, and it is even more OK to create a career on the foundation of speaking out for others. As individuals we have power, and united we can make a difference. It is OK to embrace your power and be unapologetic about what you are passionate about.

We need leaders who are committed to the equality of everybody, regardless of circumstance. We need social workers who are willing to build community coalitions based on building people up, not tearing people down. Choosing a career in social justice means that you believe that change is possible. This book can be your guide for tapping into what makes you feel passionate so that you are prepared to start your career in advocacy.

A successful career is built on many things, one of which is knowing who you are so that you are able to ask the gritty, inconvenient, more honest questions that must be asked at this moment in American history. Social workers are strong, tenacious, and resilient, and we can be the greatest voices for making change at all levels of the social welfare infrastructure. We must tap into our passions to infiltrate, agitate, and engage in acts of Graceful Revolution that support and build up the safety net for others. We must tap into our passions to resist, persist, and insist on policy changes that benefit our clients, our colleagues, and our society as a whole.

Not sure where your passions lie? Look to the personal! What are the personal concerns you have about your community? What are the things in your daily life that cause you the most apprehension, anxiety, or worry? What are the things in your daily life that cause you to feel passionate, excited, and attracted to a career in social work? Connect the dots between the challenges in your personal life and the things that light you up and make you feel passionate. Chances are you can identify the public policies that impact your life directly. If those policies affect you, then it is more than likely that the clients served by the social work profession are affected by them as well. Once you have connected with your passions, you can tap into your internal fire to make a difference and build a successful and exciting career in advocacy.

Take some time to reflect on what your passion tells you. Let your truth be your guide. Allow your enthusiasm to fuel your activism. Allow your truthful authenticity to fuel your enthusiasm. Your inner core is a powerful, positive feedback loop that is always right. Each chapter in this book gives you the opportunity to think deeply about some of the most pressing issues in social work, including poverty, mental health, LGBTQ (lesbian, gay, bisexual, transgender, queer) issues, aging, and disability. The chapters weave in information about how advocates can approach each topic from multiple lenses; for example, we discuss how environmental toxins affect mental health and how a career in health care can lead to running for office.

A few things to remember as you embark on your career in social justice advocacy. Know your core purpose and mission in the world so that you can target career opportunities that leave you feeling fulfilled and passionate. Make sure that you are prepared to leverage any combination of education and experience in order to get the job that you want. I highly recommend volunteering for nonprofit organizations with missions whose values you believe in. If you want to help children get a better education, volunteer to help read to kindergartners learning English as a second language. If you want to help the elderly access affordable health care services, volunteer at a nursing home so that you can see firsthand how people are living in later life. All of these experiences are fodder for your résumé and cover letter. Many times they lead to a permanent position when you are done with your degree. Every single job I have ever held post bachelor's degree was because I volunteered at the agency where I worked. It gave me on-the-job training so that by the time I was ready to work, they were ready to hire me.

If you believe in yourself and you stay tapped into your passion, you will get the job you want as long as you are prepared to talk about your social work training and how it makes you an ideal candidate for an advocacy position. I have been told by my colleagues that this is an incredibly "idealistic" and even an "unrealistic" statement. My response is usually to give a list of students who are making great changes in their communities because they were inspired by something they learned in one of my classes. Remember there is no perfect way to engage in advocacy, and this is one of the greatest places to engage in creativity in your work. Consider that when you are successful in your endeavors, you don't just help one person but an entire generation of humans. Thousands of people will be impacted by your willingness to pursue a career in social justice, and that is one of the greatest contributions that you can give to this great experiment in democracy.

A note about the next nine chapters:

Each chapter gives you a story of a professional social worker in the field who has engaged in advocacy as well as career opportunities in the field and examples of policies that are directly related to the chapter topic.

If you are interested in policies on a congressional level that are relevant to the topic area of a particular chapter, https://www.govtrack.us/congress/bills is a great website to consult. Each topic has a bureaucratic office at the federal level of government, and many have similar offices at the state level.

If you are interested in policies on a state level, you can go directly to your state legislative website by inputting "*name of state* and legislature" in your search engine.

If you are interested in policies on a county, city, or school board level, then you can use the search terms "*name of county* council meetings," "*name of city* council meetings," or "*name of school district* meetings."

REFERENCES

Bird, M. (2016). Social justice advocacy in the belly of the beast: An illustration of policy change for social work. *Affilia, 31*(2), 257–262.

National Association of Social Workers (NASW). (2017). *Code of ethics.* Retrieved from https://www.socialworkers.org/About/Ethics/Code-of-Ethics/Code-of-Ethics-English

POVERTY

STORIES FROM THE PROFESSION

Sonya Martinez, MSW, Salt Lake City, Utah

Maslow's "hierarchy of needs" is a fundamental concept that informs us as professional social workers. Basic needs must be provided in order for an individual to move toward self-actualization. The path of obstacles, speed bumps, and detour signs toward the fulfillment of my family's basic needs led me to social justice advocacy.

I was raised by a single mother; we relied on welfare and food stamps to fill the gaps that her various production and service work jobs could not. My biological father, who has since passed, was incarcerated and battled addiction. My older brother and his youngest son have also endured the criminal justice system and addiction.

My youth was filled with family, laughter, and deep love. It was also surrounded by a storm created by teen parenting, gangs, drugs, and the criminal justice system. My family is full of fighters, in every sense of the word. Experiencing this sparked a flame of resiliency in me.

The formative part of my life laid the foundation for social work and advocacy. Early on, I knew that I wanted a career in the helping fields. I had a resounding belief that there were complex reasons people struggled, and there was something to be done about it.

During my junior year of high school there were a handful of mentors, including a history teacher, who took an interest in me and my future. I was pushed out of my comfort zone. I was asked to volunteer on community projects. I was sent to a week-long leadership camp called Anytown. This was a space where I was given language to describe social injustices, and I discovered what equity, diversity, and inclusion looked like.

As a first-generation college student and a young mother, I struggled to attain my college education. It was during this time period I recognized that being in a helping profession did not necessarily mean I needed to go into the health care industry. I pursued a human services bachelor's degree with the understanding that I would go on to social work for graduate school.

I chose a master's degree in social work (MSW) because I was drawn to the core of social work. I was mesmerized by the concept that our field tackles social justice from micro, mezzo, and macro practice. It was a revelation that not only could we help person to person, but it was imperative to work in community and to strive for broad sweeping macro impact.

Attending a university with a heavy emphasis on clinical work often meant that I was one of a handful of students who had a persistent passion for macro social work such as policy and community and organizations. Knowing this about myself, I still chose to focus my studies and practicums in clinical work. I started to believe that in order to be a successful social worker, I should be proficient in providing therapy. Years later I would come to realize that micro and macro work are both equally important.

I graduated in 2009, during the worst recession in modern times. Competition for clinical social work jobs was fierce. I was a single mother, with a pile of debt and a desire to help. I accepted a job as a policy advocate for a local community action agency. The national Community Action Agency network was created in the 1970s as a weapon in the war on poverty. In 2009 we were still fighting many of the same battles.

During my 3 years as an advocate at Utah Community Action, I focused on poverty issues such as affordable housing, landlord–tenant law, and utility issues. I was responsible for researching and analyzing how these issues impact low-income families. It was during this time that I recognized the necessity and power in providing voice to those who are marginalized. It was also the first time I really understood that we are not powerless to injustice. I knew that my story was not in vain, and I was obligated to work with others to reduce as much harm as possible in policy making.

My colleagues and I analyzed utility policies and cases to ensure rate increases had as little impact as possible on low-income households. We fought to ensure that seniors and other low-income individuals had access to utility assistance funds. We advocated to ensure companies taking part in those same funds, like the telephone Lifeline program, did not take advantage of their customers by providing lower quality services and benefits.

In 1985 the Federal Communications Commission (FCC) created the Lifeline program, which provides discounts on phone services to low-income households. This program was created to ensure that all households have access to emergency services, connection to jobs, and communication with essential services such as health care providers. In 2010 prepaid cell-phone companies began applying to state public service commissions for the ability to allow their low-income customers to utilize the Lifeline program to obtain a prepaid cellular phone with limited wireless minutes.

I filed petitions to intervene on behalf of Community Action in multiple cases before the Utah Public Service Commission. My colleagues and I formed coalitions with other advocacy groups, met with decision makers and stakeholders, and prepared and filed written and oral testimony. Although access to utilize subsidy funds to obtain wireless service was advantageous, the services they were offering at the time were subpar. The advocacy we took part in had a direct impact on policy locally and federally. Low-income households now have more choice, access to wireless services, and significantly improved plans. Ultimately, in 2016 the FCC adopted a comprehensive reform and modernization of the program, which also addressed Internet service. These efforts were borne, at the local level, by low-income advocates from across the country.

Landlord–tenant law is a major policy concern for low-income households. As an advocate at Community Action, I worked on a number of housing bills during my tenure there. We worked on issues related to renters' rights, antidiscrimination, and foreclosure. We assessed disparate impacts in the treatment of renters with criminal histories and victims of crime. Most legislation passed consisted of compromises between landlord advocates, renter advocates, and local municipalities. We spent the years leading up to legislative sessions, working on policy to ensure voices of low-income households were reflected in the laws that were passed. Many low-income tenants would not have a vehicle to voice their concerns if housing advocates were not working toward fighting for their seat at the table.

During my time as an advocate, I also worked on a collective impact project. I led a team at Utah Community Action that prepared a proposal to create a community-based learning center in a manufactured home community. We ultimately won the proposal, which led to the creation of two sites. One site was in a community building in walking distance from five manufactured home communities, and the other was a school-based site. Residents, students, and families attending these centers had access to services that were traditionally scattered across the valley. We offered English as second language, mobile health and vision clinics, employment counseling, after-school tutoring, and numerous other services. I was responsible for management of the sites, partnership development, and service delivery.

My experience with housing advocacy and managing community-based satellite sites led me to NeighborWorks Salt Lake. The NeighborWorks national network was developed in the 1970s as a tool to fight discriminatory redlining in housing and to counter the disinvestment and blight experienced in neighborhoods with high populations of low-income and ethnic minority families. Like many social workers, after working at this career for a number of years, I found myself working in a management/administrator role.

As a program director over homeownership services in a community development organization, I manage budgets, staffing, outreach, and service delivery. We work to ensure that all people, especially the underserved, have access to affordable homeownership opportunities. Homeownership is important, as it is the primary source for asset and wealth building among U.S. families. Additionally, health, education, and life expectancy outcomes are significantly greater among people who have healthy and stable housing.

In this role I have had the opportunity to learn nonprofit accounting and budgeting, contract management, program development, marketing and outreach, and taking programs to scale. Additionally, I co-led the organization through transformational change work, including operational efficiency, social enterprise, and equity and inclusion. This opportunity has provided me with professional development as well as providing sustainability for the organization. Sustainability allows us to continue to provide comprehensive community services to those who most need it.

The thread that ties social justice advocacy and nonprofit management roles are the mezzo and macro implications of the work. In macro work, such as policy and service delivery, the results directly impact whole communities and systems at large.

Community engagement is a fundamental key to accomplishing mezzo and macro outcomes. As social workers, we should be looking toward our clients and community members to lead efforts of change. We must look to the individuals and groups we are serving as experts of their own lives. Our role is to help facilitate change guided by the people who are most affected by our society's challenges. In all of my work, I've had the opportunity to organize groups who advocate on their own behalves toward social change. They are our greatest resource.

Social justice advocacy, and macro social work in general, is for all social workers. In this vein, it is important to note that in addition to my macro work, I also maintain a part-time clinical practice. My advocacy and program management experience has been crucial in understanding the struggles my clients face. I am client-centered and recognize they are individuals affected by biopsychosocial causes. I recognize the barriers and obstacles they face. Along with their strengths, I am equipped to help them find solutions to their problems. Most importantly my direct services work informs me as an advocate and an administrator of programs and services. It is imperative that social workers at every level contribute to improving systems and creating lasting social change.

JOB DESCRIPTIONS FROM THE FIELD OF POVERTY ADVOCACY

Most states have a Community Action Partnership organization or other non-profit entities that engage in poverty advocacy. Advocating for those who are experiencing poverty is not just about focusing on income. Many advocacy careers can be built by working for organizations that advocate for food access, housing, a livable wage, or labor issues, just to name a few.

The following job descriptions are examples of opportunities that you might be interested in.

Public Policy and Strategy Manager – Washington State Community Action Partnership

Location: Olympia, Washington

Salary: 60,000–70,000

Education and Experience: 4-year degree in a related field and 6 years progressively responsible experience in public policy, project development, execution and legislative systems.

OR any combination of education and experience that would provide the applicant with the desired skills, knowledge and ability required to perform the job.

Job source: www.indeed.com

Goals of community action program:

- Assure that people have the opportunity to achieve and maintain their full potential.

- Develop strategies to prevent poverty in communities and provide a catalyst for change.

- Marshal the resources of the communities we serve to support our mission.

- Assure services and resources are available to those in poverty to meet basic needs as well as to help build skills and acquire tools that are needed to move beyond poverty.

- Assure member agencies have the capacity to carry forward the above activities.

Responsibilities:

- Develop relationships with Washington State Community Action executive directors, staff and the Legislature.

- Assist in positioning the network to take advantage of new opportunities while helping to build member capacity to respond to new opportunities. This is a current focus in the 1115 Medicaid Expansion.

- Direct forward looking legislative goals, priorities, timelines and execution strategies involving the entire WSCAP network via education, informing policy makers and leveraging the power of WSCAP.

- Coordinate and convene the WSCAP legislative committee.

- Lead the long-term campaign to address poverty in Washington State.

- Promote increased activity in civic engagement and public education by Community Action boards, staff, clients and communities at large.

- Provide advocacy trainings as needed.

- Draft talking points and letters in support of the communication and education.

- Strengthen partnerships with other aligned anti-poverty organizations and groups in Washington State.

- Design and implement a peer learning system.

- Identify and create advocacy best practices that facilitate the goals of the community.

- Develop and maintain web-based resources supporting anti-poverty efforts and public advocacy.

- Support the service and activities of contract lobbyists or other contractors as assigned by the executive director.

- Establish relationships and disseminate information to state and federal legislators, legislative staff and the governor's office.

- Increase advocacy activities by Community Action boards, staff and clients.

- Increase understanding and support by governmental agencies, legislators, community leaders and community members throughout Washington State about the value of poverty reduction efforts in their local communities.

- Increase participation and commitment by Community Action Agency board members, as a primary responsibility of their board service, to advocate on behalf of those being served.

- Promote policy changes that result in poverty.

- Increase communication and relationship building with elected officials and stakeholders.

- Develop and/or promote additional avenues for client self-advocacy.

- Strengthen relationships with other anti-poverty and social service oriented advocacy organizations to increase WSCAP and partner agency influence in guiding policy and investment of resources that helps reduce or alleviate poverty. Develop strategic alliance with key organizations.

- Create, lead, implement and continually update ambitious strategies to best position the network to meet the needs of our clients: Currently WSCAP's involvement in the 1115 Medicaid Expansion Waiver.

Statewide Poverty Impact and Equal Opportunity – Montana Department of Commerce

Salary: Not listed

Location: Montana

Education: College Degree (4 year)

Job source: www.americorps.gov

Responsibilities:

- Join the Department of Commerce to promote equal opportunity through the implementation of a statewide plan to assist in overcoming barriers to housing choice.

- This program will reduce concentrated poverty while improving access to education, affordable housing, employment opportunities, and healthcare. The Vista Member will assist in the identification or minority concentrations residing in poverty-stricken areas; evaluation of housing access to disparities and disproportionate housing needs; and identification of factors contributing to segregation and racially concentrated areas of poverty.

- Skills: leadership, community organization, environment, communications, law, recruitment, public health, team work, conflict resolution, public speaking, urban planning, education, architectural planning, writing, editing

- Service areas: Housing, community outreach, homelessness, neighborhood revitalization, health, education, community and economic development, environment, veterans

Advocacy and Field Coordinator – Poverty to Prosperity Program, Washington, DC.

Salary: Not listed

Location: Washington, D.C.

Education: Bachelor's degree with 3 years of professional experience in communications, campaigns or advocacy

Job source: www.indeed.com

Responsibilities:

- Work with Associate Director of Advocacy to develop and implement outreach strategy for a variety of campaigns as part of the team's larger field and communications strategy.

- Pitch and write original reported content for TalkPoverty.org blog featuring storytellers.

- Work on the Hands Off Campaign by handling daily submissions; outreach to storytellers for specific projects; trainings, coordination with other teams at American Progress and external partners; and developing targeted story gathering and development campaigns.

- Edit first person storyteller submissions for TalkPoverty.org.

- Pitch and vet first person storytellers for the Off Kilter Podcast.

- Assist in the continued development of both the story network and story network cohort program.

- Develop media and story sharing trainings and resources for partners and story contributors.

- Provide occasional research support for advocacy-related products.

Public Policy Analyst – Georgia Coalition Against Domestic Violence

Education and Experience: 3 years field experience working in a social justice centered organization

Salary: 40,000–49,999 per year

Job source: www.workforgood.org

Responsibilities:

- Formulate GCADV policy positions through coordinated discussion and input for GCADV staff, board, membership, key stakeholders.

- Research, analyze, and monitor public policy issues affecting domestic violence survivors and their children.

- Build alliances to promote public policy collaborations across issues such as poverty, homelessness, immigration, and human rights.

- Provide education and technical assistance to members, allies, and policymakers.

- Facilitate and inform GDADV's participation in statewide, regional, and national domestic violence policy efforts.

- Maintain strong relationships with GCADVs diverse member programs from around the state through meetings, networking, training, technical assistance, and dissemination of public policy information.

- Facilitate member programs and survivors participation in policy work.

- Work with GCADV's lobbyists to track domestic violence legislative initiatives, read and provide comments on legislative drafts provide testimony during legislative session and meet with key policy makers throughout the year.

- Represent GCADV on domestic violence task forces, workgroups, and committees as needed. Oversee and help to guide GCADV's Clemency project. Enter and analyze aggregate data for GCADV projects.

ADVOCACY FOR POVERTY: POLICY EXAMPLES

With regard to poverty legislation, states are deeply intertwined with federal policy when it comes to funding and direction from Congress for housing and Medicaid/Medicare policy. The following examples illuminate this relationship regarding the Temporary Assistance for Needy Families (TANF) program and Medicaid.

Congress is considering legislation that could affect women who receive TANF benefits, amending requirements that would force women into the workforce sooner in order to receive subsidized wages from federal and state programs.

H.R. 2842, Accelerating Individuals into the Workforce Act (2017), sponsored by Representative Carlos Curbelo (Republican from Florida's 26th congressional district), connects low-income Americans looking for work with employers looking to fill job openings, including through apprenticeships and other forms of on-the-job training. Specifically, the legislation provides funding for states to subsidize employment for a limited time for TANF recipients to provide work experience in exchange for benefits. The bill reserves $100 million from the FY18 TANF Contingency Fund to test whether states subsidizing the wage of

TANF recipients can be an effective means of helping them enter and remain in the workforce. States may subsidize up to 50% of the recipient's wage, with the remainder covered by the employer.

Each state must describe how wage subsidies will be provided and how they expect each individual to maintain employment when the subsidies end. A state shall ensure that no one is laid off from the same or a substantially similar job to create positions for such participants.

Finally, a state has to submit a report that specifies the number of individuals whose employment is subsidized, the structure of state activities, the percentage of recipients who received a subsidy who are in unsubsidized employment during the second quarter after the subsidies ended, and the median earning of recipients after the subsidies end.

Status: Passed the House, in the Senate (Nov. 2017)

According to the Medicaid and Children's Health Insurance Program (CHIP) Payment and Access Commission (2017), several states have asked or are planning to ask the Centers for Medicare and Medicaid Services (CMS) for permission to impose work requirements as a condition of Medicaid eligibility through Section 1115 research and demonstration waiver authority. Although there are currently no work requirements in any state Medicaid program, other federal programs require participation in work activities as a condition of eligibility, including TANF. These requirements can be devastating for the working poor.

Ohio HB 49 – State Budget amendments

Sub HB 49 limits Medicaid expansion coverage to Ohioans who are 55 years and older; employed; have intensive health needs; or are enrolled in school, occupational training, or substance abuse treatment.

Such work requirements ignore the fact that 43% of Medicaid expansion enrollees were already employed in 2014–2015 and that 75% of those not employed were looking for work. It is that group – job seekers – who will be hurt by these changes. But others could easily fall outside of eligibility under these provisions: a husband who cannot work because he is taking care of an ill wife or someone who suffers from a mental illness not included as an "intensive health need."

Despite the passage of the budget, limits have not yet been imposed as of November 2017. Because of the upheaval in the federal government regarding the Affordable Care Act (ACA), Ohio is still awaiting guidance about how they will be able to proceed with this potentially catastrophic policy.

Status: The budget became effective June 29, 2017; the Medicaid issue is still in political limbo.

REFERENCES

H.R. 2842 – 115th Congress: Accelerating Individuals into the Workforce Act. (2017). Retrieved from https://www.govtrack.us/congress/bills/115/hr2842

Medicaid and CHIP Payment and Access Commission (MACPAC). (2017, October). *Work as a condition of Medicaid eligibility: Key take-aways from TANF* (Issue Brief). https://www.macpac.gov/publication/work-as-a-condition-of-medicaid-eligibility -key-take-aways-from-tanf

CHILD WELFARE

STORIES FROM THE PROFESSION

Beth Davenport, MSW, San Diego, CA

I grew up in New Orleans in the late 1980s and early 1990s with a single mother who was a home health care nurse. Rather than leave me with a babysitter, she used to take me with her to care for her patients who were dying of AIDS. (This was before HIPAA, of course.) Even at that early age, I understood the magnitude of the AIDS epidemic and its effect on the LGBT community. To memorialize my favorite patient, Joe, I named my new cat after him. I've taken this experience with me as I've grown into an adult and often reflect on it as motivation to continue my fight to achieve social justice in society.

One of my first jobs after completing my bachelor's degree was as mental health technician on a psychiatric unit. I held this position for 3 years while attending graduate school where I was pursuing a master's degree in social work (MSW). I rotated through each of the six specialized units operated by the hospital: adult, adolescent, acute, geriatric, eating disorder, and substance abuse. This experience was invaluable as I was allowed to directly interact with patients, many of whom had diagnoses that I had only read about in textbooks. I was also able to work with a multidisciplinary team of nurses, social workers, and psychiatrists, which was a rare opportunity to have had at such an early stage in my career.

My time as a mental health technician was also an eye-opening experience. I witnessed the revolving door of chronically mentally ill patients, primarily people of color, with low income and either in an unstable housing situation or with no housing at all. It was heartbreaking to witness. They would come back time and time again, suffering from the same unresolved issues that never truly got addressed. It was here that I got my first glimpse into a professional setting how individuals with less privilege were treated differently.

This job also helped shape me into the social worker that I am today. It was during my time as a mental health technician that I realized I wanted to be the kind of social worker that could go home at night and lay my head on my pillow, knowing I did everything possible for each client with whom I worked. I was moving closer to realizing that I was meant to be an advocate who fights for the rights of others.

In the second year of the MSW program, I was assigned an internship at a community mental health clinic in Baton Rouge, Louisiana. During my time there, I met with low-income clients, primarily people of color and those living without insurance. My field supervisor, Bruce, is to this day the best supervisor I've ever had. His passions were equality and cultural competency. A lot of his ideas and systems continue to guide me in my work today.

Looking back at the letter of intent I wrote for the MSW program, I could see my passion for social justice was evident all those years ago. The letter spoke to my aspiration to "make a difference and improve cultural competency in community-based organizations" and to my desire to "effect policy change." Having confirmed the direction I wanted my career to take, I then needed to figure out where to focus my efforts.

After receiving my MSW degree in December 1999, I moved to San Diego to start my career as a social worker. My first position was at a private foster care and adoption agency that had offices in San Diego, Riverside, San Bernardino, and Los Angeles counties. I worked there for 11 years and held various positions, including social worker, teen services coordinator, director of quality assurance, and executive director of adoptions. During my time at this agency, I worked with many foster youth who identified as LGBT. It's no secret that youth need to feel socially, emotionally, and physically safe and supported in order to thrive. These youth did not feel safe anywhere. The rejection they experienced by their biological parents, foster parents, teachers, therapists, social workers, and peers was heartbreaking.

I had finally found my focus and a place to "make a difference and improve cultural competency in community-based organizations" both on a micro and a macro level. Through the support of the leadership of the agency, I continued working with LGBT youth and took on the role as a champion for LGBT competency at this agency by changing policies and procedures so that they were inclusive of LGBT foster parents and youth.

The first of many changes included the redesign of the website to include language and photos that were inclusive of people of color and LGBT families. This was before marriage equality (i.e., before the 2015 U.S. Supreme Court decision that guaranteed the fundamental right for same-sex couples to marry), so all of the parent-related forms were revised to be inclusive of LGBT parents. Additionally, an LGBT 101 training was added to the foster parent training curriculum. Among other things, it explained each letter of the acronym *LGBT* and dispelled common myths associated with being LGBT. Additionally, LGBT-inclusive information was added to all of the other foster parent trainings.

These changes were implemented in 2002 before AB 458 was passed in California, protecting LGBT youth and foster parents from discrimination and requiring training for foster care staff and foster families. The leadership of the agency received pushback from some board members, staff, and foster parents. Despite the opposition, I was able to help them understand that this was a civil rights issue for the LGBT community, and consequently they followed through with the changes. I had my first achievement as an advocate for others, and it felt good.

Now that I had a focus and knew that I could effect change on a larger scale, I just needed to figure out the next steps. On a whim, I decided to submit proposals to be a presenter at youth-focused conferences around the country. If accepted, I would present information about how to create an inclusive environment for LGBT youth and foster parents. Much to my surprise, nearly every proposal was accepted. The training curriculum that I had developed for the foster family and adoption agency ended up being shared with foster parents and staff of community organizations across the country. I was really making a difference and improving cultural competency in community-based organizations now!

In 2004, I was asked to sit on a committee to assist in the development of a permanent supportive housing program for LGBT youth in San Diego who were homeless. The initial phase of this project was to conduct a needs assessment that collected qualitative information related to the cultural competency of child welfare staff and administrators who work with LGBT youth. It also examined the experiences and opinions of LGBT youth regarding their treatment while under the care of the child welfare system. The results were shameful. The needs assessment confirmed that foster care staff and administrators knew almost nothing about how to create a safe and welcoming environment for LGBT youth, and LGBT youth communicated that they didn't feel safe.

It was through the youth housing partnership that I formed a relationship with the San Diego LGBT Community Center. Six years later, I accepted a position as the chief operating officer (COO) at the center, where I still work today. The center provides direct services to the many different facets of the LGBT community, including men, women, youth, seniors, families, LGBT Latino community members and their families, as well as those struggling with HIV. Last year, the center provided more than 70,000 direct service visits to San Diego community members. I found my dream job.

One of my roles as COO is overseeing the youth housing program. Now in its 11th year, the program has served over 100 homeless LGBT and/or HIV-positive youth. Incredibly, over 80% of the youth who live at the Sunburst Youth Housing Program leave the program to stable housing and don't return to homelessness.

Occasionally I find myself crossing paths at the San Diego LGBT Community Center with one of the LGBT youth that I worked with years ago. They often greet me with a huge hug and share how their life is progressing. Several of them are paying it forward by being advocates for LGBT youth and the transgender community. Their courage truly warms my heart.

I am very aware that I am privileged based purely on who I was when I was born, being both white and heterosexual. I also realize that my straightness often makes me one of the most powerful voices in the room when advocating for the LGBT community. In my role as COO and in my personal life, I use this privilege every chance I get to help others.

Fifteen years ago, I became a social justice warrior by becoming an ally to LGBT youth, and it was one of the best decisions I ever made.

JOB DESCRIPTIONS FROM THE FIELD OF CHILD WELFARE ADVOCACY

Public Safety and Community Justice Manager – Hollywood, CA

Salary: No salary posted

Requirements:

- Bachelor's degree in urban studies, public policy, political science, community development or related field required. Plus 3 years of management experience.

- Commitment to social and economic justice including community organizing, human rights community development and empowerment.

Responsibilities:

- Develop a year-long community engagement effort and develop a public safety plan for MacArthur Park area and surrounding area.

- Work in partnership with Youth Policy Institute (YPI) Chief Community Development Officer, Director of Research and Evaluation, and project research partner.

- Keep detailed documentation of all program qualitative and quantitative data gathering efforts for a full community assessment.

- Maintain and strengthen community partnership relationships and serve as a liaison with community leaders, community organizations and school leadership, public agencies and residents to assist in sustaining public interest in the project.

- Develop a 2- and 3-year implementation plan and work to ensure that key strategies are implemented and partner and stakeholders are engaged.

- Manage subcontracts to ensure key outcomes are being met and that there is appropriate data and documentation available for all reports.

- Oversee development of program materials such as flyers, brochures and any type of communication documents in conjunction with YPI's communication team.

- Work to identify potential additional funding resources to help advance agenda of YPI and Byrne Criminal Justice and Promise Zone initiatives.

- Represent YPI at meetings and events as it relates to public safety issues.

- Meet with community development officer regularly to ensure program outcomes and that goals are met in a timely manner.

Job source: www.indeed.com

Policy Specialist Education (for State Legislature) – Denver, CO

Education Requirement: Bachelor's degree plus 5 years' experience

Job Description: The policy education specialist will take interest in post-secondary education concerns. They will conduct research, analyze data and interpret and identify policy implications. They will make recommendations to policy drafts and describe potential policy options. The policy specialist will work closely with special interest groups, government officials, and the private sector to promote and advocate for the national conference of state legislature's position. Uses creativity to share a variety of complex information through verbal presentation, workshops, videotapes, letters, memos, newsletters and articles. Using clear and concise writing the policy education specialist will contribute to publications including books, magazine articles and long reports. Assists with project development and advocates for continued prospects for support. Adapts method of information dissemination for a variety of audiences including constituents.

Salary: $4,428 per month

Location: Denver, Colorado

Child Welfare Program Analyst – Richmond, VA

Salary: $43,892–70,000

Job source: www.jobs.virginia.gov

Education: Bachelor's degree with major course work in social science, public health, public policy, or other related field; equivalent relevant training and experience may be considered.

Responsibilities:

- Joining the Maternal and Child Health Unit within the Division of Health Care Services to provide guidance and oversight for the foster Care and Adoption Assistance programs for those served through the DMAS contracted Managed Care Organizations

- Work closely with state and local departments of social services, DMAS Staff, Virginia Medicaid contracted MCOs and interested stakeholders to ensure that foster care and adoption assistance children have necessary medical and behavioral health services

- Responsible for program development and policy development

- Represent the department at FC/AA stakeholder and advisory committee meetings either on ad hoc basis or through participation and leadership on work groups, task forces focused on population, providing education training, technical assistance and guidance to Departments of Social Services, foster care and adoption assistance parents, etc.

Policy Specialist, Child Welfare – Maryland Courts

Location: Annapolis, Maryland

Salary: $60,120

Education and Experience: Five (5) years of related work experience, which must include 3 years of experience in the area of Child Welfare or court experience in the Juvenile arena.

Job source: www.mdcourts.gov

Responsibilities: The Child Welfare Policy Specialist works with the Foster Care Court Improvement Program (FCCIP) in implementing and furthering its goal to improve the Judiciary's handling of Children in Need of Assistance (CINA) and related Guardianship and Adoption cases. The Policy Specialist facilitates the implementation of new program initiatives and best practices as they relate to CINA and related Guardianship and Adoption cases throughout the State. Provides technical assistance to Maryland courts on child welfare law. Researches child welfare issues and maintains expertise in child welfare law and state and federal policy. Helps coordinate and provide technical assistance to the Permanency Planning Liaisons throughout the State. Serves as an active liaison with other child welfare justice partners in the Executive branch. The Policy Specialist performs other duties as assigned by the Director of Juvenile and Family Services.

Adoption Specialist – Department of Social and Health Service, Wenatchee, Washington

Job source: www.governmentjobs.com

Description
Adoption Specialist – Social Service Specialist 3

Do you want the ability to impact families in a positive way? Bring your professional knowledge, excellent communications skills and emotional intelligence to work with a career at Children's Administration (CA).

In this role of Adoption Specialist you will ensure timely permanency outcomes for all children on their caseload with their primary emphasis on adoption.

Some of what you'll do:

- Meet all casework management directives required by law, policy, and other mandates

- Provision of assessment, service planning, casework, court and teaming services on assigned cases

- Coordinate with relatives, social workers, GAL/CASAs, assistant Attorney Generals, private agencies, relative or foster caregivers, medical/educational professionals and other community professionals

- Assessment, delivery of services and permanency planning that is inclusive of immediate family, extended family, kin, and children

- Develop strength-based and client-involved service plans

- Provide case management services and education regarding the adoption of children with special needs

- Identify and initiate services to maintain adoptive placements

- Evaluate need for continued out-of-home care and long-term goals

- Assess complex situations and develop plans and advise best ways to protect children

- Develop initial and ongoing safety assessments and safety plans

- Prepare legal documents necessary for adoption finalization

- Provide accurate and timely entries into FamLink

We're looking for professionals who have successfully demonstrated:

- Knowledge of DSHS/CA policies and procedures, including knowledge of federal and state statutes governing child welfare and adoption work

- Implement culturally-relevant, ADA-sensitive and individualized service plans

- Engaging children and families under difficult circumstances, to gather information to make accurate and precise decisions

- Ability to identify problems, develop and implement solutions

- Communicating information both orally and in writing so others will understand

- Ability to remain calm when being confronted and to develop constructive and cooperative working relationships with others

- Excellent verbal and written communication skills

- Successfully managing competing priorities

Who should apply?

Professionals with a Bachelor's Degree in social services, human services, behavioral sciences or a related field AND three or more years of paid social service experience which includes two years' assessing risk and safety to children and providing direct family-centered practices services.

Note: A practicum will be substituted for the one year of paid social service experience. A Master's Degree in social services, human services, behavioral sciences, or a related field and two years of paid social service experience.

Degrees must be obtained from an accredited institution; please attach a copy of your college transcripts, cover letter and resume to this application.

Supplemental Information:

Prior to a new hire, a background check including criminal record history may be conducted. Information from the background check will not necessarily preclude employment but will be considered in determining the applicant's suitability and competence to perform in the job. This announcement may be used to fill multiple vacancies. Employees driving on state business must have a valid driver's license. Employees driving a privately owned vehicle on state business must have liability insurance on the privately owned vehicle.

Washington State Department of Social and Health Services is an equal opportunity employer and does not discriminate on the basis of age, sex, sexual orientation, gender, gender identity/expression, marital status, race, creed, color, national origin, religion or beliefs, political affiliation, military status, honorably discharged veteran, Vietnam Era; recently separated or other protected veteran status, the presence of any sensory, mental, physical disability or the use of a trained dog guide or service animal by a person with a disability, equal pay or genetic information. Persons requiring accommodation in the application process or this job announcement in an alternative format may contact a Recruiter at (360) 725-5810. Applicants who are deaf or hard of hearing may call through Washington Relay Service by dialing 7-1-1 or 1-800-833-6384.

ADVOCACY FOR CHILD WELFARE: POLICY EXAMPLES

The prevailing laws regarding child welfare originate from the Child Abuse Prevention and Treatment Act (CAPTA), which was originally signed in 1974. This law has been amended many times since then, most recently to address issues of human trafficking and substance abuse.

CAPTA was reauthorized on May 29, 2015, by the Justice for Victims of Trafficking Act of 2015 (P.L. 114-22) and on July 22, 2016, by the Comprehensive Addiction and Recovery Act of 2016 (P.L. 114-198) (Child Welfare Information Gateway, 2017).

Although much of this looks like just a bunch of numbers, it is important that advocates understand which bill numbers social welfare policies are connected to so that you can search them on the Internet and reference them in your advocacy work.

The Child Welfare Information Gateway is a great place to retrieve federal- and state-level information regarding child welfare policies. You can find the gateway at https://www.childwelfare.gov/topics/systemwide/laws-policies.

REFERENCE

Child Welfare Information Gateway. (2017). *About CAPTA: A legislative history*. Retrieved from https://www.childwelfare.gov/pubs/factsheets/about

HEALTH CARE

STORIES FROM THE PROFESSION

Kathryn Rehner, MSW, LMSW, Mississippi

Social Work Advocacy in Mississippi

My name is Kathryn Rehner. I'm 27, a native Mississippian, social worker, community organizer, one-time political candidate, and a pragmatic optimist who believes that change can happen for people and within systems—even in Mississippi.

To understand my practice and the role advocacy plays in my work and life, you have to understand some things about Mississippi. Mississippi ranks poorly in nearly all health outcomes nationwide. According to the 2016 *America's Health Rankings* annual report, Mississippi ranks 50th as the nation's most challenged state. Some of the challenges include high prevalence of smoking and low birthweight, and a high percentage of children living in poverty. In addition, Mississippi has a 17% uninsured rate, a 35% obesity rate, and 6.5% of Mississippians are unemployed.

Such unflattering statistics, and others like them, are the direct result of decisions and legislative priorities, perpetuated by policies, systems, and practices that both intentionally and unintentionally make it difficult for vulnerable populations to obtain services. For example, a community-wide survey conducted by the University of Southern Mississippi School of Social Work in 2013 found that the greatest barrier Hattiesburg families faced to enroll in Medicaid and the Children's Health Insurance Plan (CHIP) was transportation. Despite this rather evident reality (or because of it?), the child support office—previously sensibly co-located with the food stamp office—was relocated in 2017 to West Hattiesburg, a more affluent community beyond city bus routes. The Medicaid office was similarly relocated beyond public transportation access, making it substantially more difficult for families to get the services they need, services that the Mississippi State Legislature view as poverty-perpetuating "handouts."

Social services in general have long been under state-level assault. For years, Mississippi's legislature has rendered Medicaid more and more difficult for children and families to access under the guise of fiscal responsibility. In Mississippi, Medicaid is funded 74.4% by the federal government, making the state share virtually insignificant in comparison to the benefits received. Still, the state refused to adopt changes that would reduce the burden on families to obtain and retain health coverage. Reasonable and helpful changes, such as providing a true online application process and automatic renewal, were not adopted by Mississippi when the opportunity arose through the implementation of the Affordable Care Act. Such systems issues, making life unnecessarily difficult for hundreds of thousands of average Mississippians, are pervasive.

Why Mississippi Needs Advocates

Blatant disregard for the general welfare, a consistent refusal to serve and represent all persons in our communities, both directly and indirectly threatens my clients and those I have committed to work for daily. Decisions about education, health care, and social services clearly point to who and what the state legislature prioritizes. In 2016, Mississippi passed one of the most egregious anti-LGBTQ laws in the United States: House Bill 1523, disingenuously characterized as protection for "religious freedom." HB 1523 states that no discriminatory actions can be taken against anyone who holds these main values: marriage should be recognized as the union between one man and one woman; sexual relationships are properly reserved for marriage; and gender is immutable from the biological sex assigned at birth. The law allows citizens and business owners to refuse service to anyone based on their Christian convictions regarding sex, marriage, and gender.

The Mississippi Legislature also passed Senate Bill 2469, the "Blue Lives Matter" bill, which provides enhanced penalties under Mississippi hate crime law to include persons convicted of aggravated assault or other crimes against an officer or other first responder. It enhances penalties in such situations up to double the standard sentence with no early parole. While Mississippi has, fortunately, been so far spared from killing incidents like those in communities such as Ferguson, St. Louis, Chicago, and Baltimore, it is not surprising that the legislature's response is to ignore the possibility of abusive police behavior and instead secure police power.

State priorities are seen not only in actions (laws passed), but in failures to act. In the last legislative session, an equal pay for equal work bill was brought to committee to protect women from pay discrimination. Unfortunately, this bill never made it out of committee. Mississippi has failed to fully fund public education for nearly a decade, resulting in generations of children who, through no fault of their own, are unprepared for higher education or the workforce. In the same sense, Mississippi does not mandate kindergarten attendance and does not fund pre-K education. Viewing public education as a burdensome expense instead of a prudent investment in the state's future, government has chosen to ignore the many benefits of quality schooling, from early children to higher education.

The decision most directly detrimental to my clients and to the health status of Mississippians was our governor's decision to opt out of Medicaid expansion. In 2013, Governor Bryant claimed that Medicaid expansion would bankrupt the state, when in reality, as the poorest state in America, Mississippi would have received nearly $20 for every $1 spent to expand Medicaid. So instead of creating jobs and stimulating the economy, the legislature chose to leave hundreds of thousands of Mississippians uninsured and without access to the medical care they need to be successful and contributing members of society. For many, life-saving prescriptions are not an option, mental health care is not an option, and standard preventative screenings are not an option. These are my clients. They are the people I have worked to find resources or alternative care for over the past 4 years, and they are the reason I decided to run for Mississippi House of Representative for House District 102.

Social Work and Health Care

For the past 4 years, I have been working in health care outreach and enrollment through grant-funded programs. My first position was working as the program coordinator for the City of Hattiesburg's E³ (Educate, Enroll, Empower) Health Initiative. This program was funded through the National League of Cities to help educate and enroll children and families in Medicaid/CHIP. This grant targeted three elementary schools in the Hattiesburg Public School District. Within this target area, we estimated that there were approximately 19,000 residents. Of those 19,000 residents, there were nearly 6,000 eligible for health coverage who were not insured. The goal for this project was to reduce the uninsured rate by 50%, that is, to enroll 3,000 persons in health coverage over the grant's

18-month period. We did just that. Knowing that transportation was the primary barrier in obtaining coverage, I developed an outreach and enrollment model that brought the application process to eligible populations or what I call the "lived spaces" where people spend their time. Instead of asking a single mom to drive 30 minutes to the Medicaid office across town, we began offering enrollment opportunities at Women, Infants, and Children (WIC) Centers, health department clinics, schools, food pantries, after-school programs, and community centers. We made the enrollment process simple, quick, and convenient – doing everything that the state was not doing.

E^3 empowered people to know and understand their health care rights. For the first time, a trusted agency, in this case, a city government, was telling them that they had a right to health care. Many people I spoke to had been denied coverage by Medicaid without explanation, leaving them to assume there were no health coverage options available. When I would speak to a family and let them know that they were indeed eligible and that they had been wrongfully denied coverage (which happens far too frequently), they were empowered to stand up for themselves and demand what they knew they deserved. E^3 walked with them through that process. I accompanied families to the Medicaid office to speak with case workers on their behalf, reported instances where regional offices had failed to comply with federal Medicaid mandates, and educated each family about their rights under the law. The work I did with the City of Hattiesburg through the E^3 Health Initiative extended beyond micro to mezzo practice, as I worked to create a network of agencies and organizations in our community that integrated health coverage into individual agency cultures. This network focused on making health access a shared responsibility rather than an individual one. The success of my program resulted in roughly $2.5 million for health access funding in south Mississippi over the next 4 years, including my current federal Navigator grant program, "MS Health Access Collaborative" (MHAC).

As the project director for the MHAC, I am implementing the same model to build sustainable access to health care for vulnerable and underserved populations in the 24 southernmost counties of the state. One of two Navigator entities in Mississippi, MHAC's primary focus is enrolling individuals and families in health care coverage under the Affordable Health Care Act ("Obamacare"). Prior to January 20, 2017, our only concern as Navigators was what Mississippi would do to limit access to eligible children and families. Now, however, Obamacare is being attacked on all sides by the Trump administration. We have so far managed to escape repeal and replace bills but must fight executive orders that discriminate against women and their access to birth control, increase premiums for consumers who depend on government assistance, lower the cost for unregulated insurance plans, and cut funding for outreach and education programs like mine. Many of our clients depend on the Affordable Care Act to have coverage that is literally saving their lives. They live on fixed incomes and are not eligible for Medicare. Paying more than $75 per month for health coverage is simply not an option for them. The fight goes on, and no doubt attacks will continue as long as a presidential administration and Congress are hostile to the general welfare of average Americans, but unlike many other states, the Mississippi Legislature will not thwart these attacks from the federal government or protect Mississippians from losing access to health coverage.

Social Workers in Public Office

As social workers, we have relationships with people and communities who are most impacted by legislative decisions. Governor Bryant's decision to opt out of Medicaid expansion was easy for him because he has never had to look someone in the face and tell them that they are not eligible for coverage. Every day I have to tell someone they will not be able to get the help they need to pay for medical care. I have to explain to them that Mississippi makes it hard for average people to get health coverage because our government views health care as a privilege rather than a right. It is these daily conversations with clients that demand a response, demand a voice. Social workers are uniquely positioned to be that voice for communities. So, in July 2017, I announced my candidacy for Representative of House District 102, to be a voice for all those who have been ignored by the Mississippi Legislature.

As a social worker, I go to work every day to create solutions to real problems people face in our community, whether that is a student intern who is struggling to balance school, bills, and two jobs or a single mom who doesn't have reliable transportation to get to a doctor's appointment for her little girl. These are real problems that I am tired of putting Band-Aids on because our state legislature insists on ignoring the needs of average Mississippians. Although we knew the cards were stacked against us in this special election, I changed the conversation to one of "putting people first." On October 3, 2017, 3,000 of the roughly 13,000 voters determined who would go to the state capital as our Representative. Even though I lost to the Republican candidate, my campaign was always about more than one election. It was just the beginning. Creating real change for our clients in Mississippi is a battle we will have to fight every day, at every opportunity. We have to build a movement that at once encompasses elections and goes beyond them. We have to organize and activate people, citizens, and my campaign was a catalyst for renewed political and civic engagement in Hattiesburg.

In a place like Mississippi, it is easy to become discouraged, to feel that meaningful change will never come because hate, corruption, discrimination, and bad ideology still have such a stranglehold on the culture. In both politics and in social work practice, too many give up in fatigue and despair. But now more than ever we have to fight against the forces of reaction, fight for doing the things that others say cannot be done. If we as social work advocates do not tell our clients' stories, if we are not their voice and help them discover their own voices, if we fail to be their advocates, then who else will fight for them? Our profession was born in struggle, and for more than a century has struggled to advance the cause of social justice, in big and small ways, at every level and in every venue of practice. We stand on the right side of history. As the next generation of social workers, it is your responsibility to continue that most important tradition of promoting social justice and social change on behalf of our clients.

JOB DESCRIPTIONS FROM THE FIELD OF HEALTH CARE ADVOCACY

Health Educator – Nationwide

Education Required: Bachelor's degree in health education/health promotion/related field

Salary: $53,070 (May 2016). Salaries range from $30,400–$95,730.

Job Description: Health educators work to determine program efficacy and the needs of those they serve by analyzing data. These individuals must be comfortable with public speaking as they often facilitate discussion and lead programs related to health conditions. Excellent writing skills are needed as these individuals create and provide the community with written health materials. These individuals may also advocate by writing proposals for funding to develop and improve community health programs. Additionally, employers may provide on the job training on the topics each health educator will specialize in. Health educators understand that culture plays a role in health behaviors and outcomes. They use their skills and knowledge to improve community health through education and advocacy.

Job source: https://www.bls.gov

Office of Rural Health and Primary Care Director – State Program Administrator Manager Principal

Education: Bachelor's degree and 5 years of experience

Salary: $79,866–114,568 annually

Location: St. Paul, Minnesota

Job source: https://careers.mn.gov

Responsibilities: Work to provide direction and leadership for statewide support to assist the health care safety net that assists 1,400,000 Minnesotans. Provide policy research, planning, analysis and recommendations related to Minnesota's health care delivery, safety net system, rural health, urban underserved areas, health care workforce and medical education concerns. Assist with policy programs and partnerships on health reform for the Minnesota health care system and safety net system to ensure its availability to underserved populations. Coordinate program administration to meet the goals of the department. Manage the sections budget including state and federal appropriations, federal and private grant funding and Medicaid funding. Plan and monitor spending from various accounts within the budget.

Director of State Policy and Advocacy – American Kidney Fund

Average Salary: $110,000–115,000 per year

Education and Experience: College degree required, no mention of advanced degree. 7–10 years of experience required.

Job source: https://www.indeed.com

Responsibilities:

- Recommend to the Vice President of Government Affairs the public policy and legislative positions and strategies that AKF should undertake at the state level and develop a proactive AKF state strategy.

- Work directly with state legislatures and state executive branch agencies. This includes working with key healthcare policy makers, including members of legislative committees with jurisdiction over healthcare, as well as the Departments of Insurance and other state agencies and executive departments tasked with overseeing state healthcare programs.

- Collaborate with colleagues in the Office of Government Affairs to develop grassroots action plan that strategically engages AKF patient-advocates to achieve desired policy outcomes.

- Identify key states and monitor activity with these state legislatures and government agencies as well as insurance company activity with regard to issues affecting people with end stage renal disease.

- Develop and implement proactive strategies and plans of action aimed at insurance companies, state government officials and agencies to facilitate AKF-desired outcomes, including representing AKF to state officials, comment letters, position descriptions, etc.

- Develop relationships with key state officials and stakeholders, as well as with other advocacy organizations.

- Coordinate with the AKF director of government affairs to engage with the National Association of Insurance Commissioners on an on-going basis.

- Communicate effectively and work closely with colleagues in the AKF Office of Government Affairs and other AKF colleagues, as well as the AKF advocacy network.

- Collaborate with AKF's public relations agency of record to provide needed information to execute effective statute-level media campaigns.

- Assess outside counsel and lobbying need within each state and manage these resources appropriately.

Legislative and Policy Strategist – Center for State Policy Helping Family Physicians Advance Health

Salary: No salary listed

Location: Washington, D.C.

Experience and Education:

- Bachelor's degree (graduate degree preferred) in an academic field directly related and essential to the job or through equivalent work experience, plus at least two to four years related experience. State government relations experience with an interest in health care policy, or health care policy experience with an interest in state government relations helpful.

The incumbent must possess a solid understanding of state-federal relations and roles in the policy-making process. Knowledge of state health care issues, excellent communication skills, and strong research and writing skills.

Responsibilities:

- The Legislative and Policy Strategist will assist the Manager, Center for State Policy in analysis of state health policy, track state legislation on issues affecting family medicine, and provide research for AAFP's chapters in support of their governmental advocacy programs. The Legislative and Policy Strategist will also assist the Manager of Strategic Advocacy Communications in federal grassroots engagements. The position is an integral part of the planning process of advocacy-related meetings. The position will report to the Manager, Center for State Policy. Approximately 14 days travel per year. Other duties as assigned.

State Legislative Analyst – Government and Pharmacy Affairs

Education and Experience: Bachelor's degree in political science, public policy, government, or related field and 3 years of state legislative experience.

Location: Alexandria, Virginia

Job source: https://workforcenow.adp.com

About the organization: For 30 years the Academy of Managed Care Pharmacy has been the nation's leading professional association dedicated to increasing patient access to affordable medicines and improving health outcomes. Our 8,000 pharmacists, physicians, nurses, and other practitioners manage medication therapies for over 270 million Americans.

Responsibilities:
This position works within the Department of Government and Pharmacy Affairs at AMCP and leads our state legislative tracking and reporting needs. Working closely with the Director of Legislative Affairs, this role is responsible for identifying, tracking, and monitoring state legislation related to AMCP issues. You will also research, analyze, and summarize legislation, draft comment letters, briefs and other issue related correspondence for target audiences. AMCP is a highly collaborative environment and seeks candidates that enjoy working in an open office environment and cooperative atmosphere.

- Providing timely responses to member requests, identifying important issues and the connection to AMCP policy; develop advocacy materials and grassroots communications

- Create and maintain legislative tracking charts and contribute to AMCP written member communications

Health Care – Public Health Educator

Location: Dallas, Texas

Company: Parkland Hospital

Job source: https://www.parklandcareers.com

Looking for your next opportunity? If so, choose Parkland and discover what a meaningful job feels like. Whether you work directly with patients or use your talent to support our care, you'll be part of a team that's providing valuable health services to Dallas County residents. And here, you'll have the opportunity to put all your skills to work, and the support to grow and advance in your job and your field. Step into a career that will make a substantial difference for our patients—and for you. We blend cultures, talents, and experience into an exemplary health and hospital system. Parkland has earned distinction as one of America's Best Hospitals by *U.S. News & World Report* every year since 1994.

Responsible for the assessment of health education needs, developing and presenting appropriate educational materials, continuously evaluating program activities and revising as needed to ensure a quality health education program.

Education:

- Must have a Bachelor's degree in Public Health, Health Education, Community Health Education or related field.

Experience:

- Must have two years of experience in the development and implementation of health education programs, community outreach, and public speaking.

Equivalent Education and/or Experience:

- May have an equivalent combination of education and/or experience in lieu of specific education and/or experience as stated above.

Certification/Registration/Licensure:

- None

Skills or Special Abilities:

- Must be able to communicate effectively with all levels of staff and management.

- Must be able to demonstrate a working knowledge of training methods and techniques, including the group facilitation process.

- Must be able to demonstrate excellent writing and communication skills.

- Must demonstrate knowledge and skill in working with a diverse population.

- Must be organized, detail oriented and able to work independently.

- Must demonstrate patient centered/patient valued behaviors.

- Must be able to demonstrate a working knowledge of PC operations, and be able to use word processing, spreadsheet, presentation, and database software.

Case Manager – Pueblo, Colorado

Salary: $19.41/hour (40 hr work week)

Job source: https://www.health.solutions

Qualifications: Bachelor's Degree in Social Work, Psychology, Education or closely related field required. Experience in conducting clinical interviews and triage assessments, family case management, and community systems navigation desired. Experience working with children/families as well as school systems preferred. Valid Colorado Driver License and access to transportation during working hours required.

Other: Experience working with a multi-disciplinary team. CAC eligible and ability to speak Spanish desired but not required. Computer proficiency required. Must be a self-starter, self-motivator and possess exceptional time management, presentation and documentation skills.

Responsibilities: Provision of supportive services to children/adolescents/families who are at high risk of being hospitalized. The Case Manager will provide support with the goal of assisting children/adolescents/families through crises. Services may be provided in home in conjunction with services at Health Solutions or at other locations in the community that provide a setting of natural support for the client such as the school setting. Duties can include transportation of clients, provision of brief supportive therapy sessions and case management services. The Case Manager will also be required to perform evaluation and triage duties on children and families that present at the agency for enrollment into treatment.

Desired Attributes:

- Is adaptable to change in the workplace and uses change as an opportunity for innovation and creativity.

- Takes ownership of problems, has ability to brainstorm different problem resolution paths, uses sound judgment in selecting solutions to problems, and demonstrates consistent follow-through.

- Has job knowledge and skills to perform the fundamental job functions and is able and willing to assume greater responsibility over time regarding the scope of work.

- Has the ability to inspire and model collaborative teamwork.

- Demonstrates an understanding of customer service regarding accommodation, politeness, helpfulness, trust building, appropriate boundaries, and flexibility.

Job Duties:

- Identifying stressors and precursors which led up to the current crisis

- Identifying coping mechanisms and natural supports that may be available

- Attend school staffings and provide support to the school system

- Provide education re: mental health diagnosis

- Enhancement of problem-solving skills

- Providing consistent support and availability until the child/adolescent/family has achieved a higher level of functioning

- Teaching the child/adolescent/family about available community resources including peer support activities

- Linking the child/adolescent/family with community resources

- Linking the child/adolescent/family with the schools

- Helping the child/adolescent/family to make and keep scheduled appointments with medical doctors

- Providing/arranging transportation for scheduled appointments

- Provide support to remain in home and community to avoid more restrictive, disruptive out of home placements

- Keep accurate, complete and up-to-date records with 100% compliance with Health Solutions standards

- Maintain competency and proficiency with the electronic health record

- Perform other job-related duties assigned by the Director or his/her designee

ADVOCACY FOR HEALTH CARE: POLICY EXAMPLES

As mentioned previously, there are many ways that policies intersect across levels of government and topic area. Health care is certainly one of those places. The two major health care policy opportunities are under the Affordable Care Act and usually involve Medicaid and Medicare. Social justice advocates who understand the expansiveness of Medicaid and Medicare and how health care budgets are directly affected by these two programs are worth their weight in gold in the policy arena.

Coverage gap for adults – In states that are not expanding Medicaid, the Kaiser Family Foundation estimates that nearly 2.5 million poor uninsured adults fall into the "coverage gap" that results from a lack of Medicaid expansion (Garfield & Damico, 2017).

Accessibility to rural health care – According to the American Hospital Association (2017), rural hospitals provide essential health care services to nearly 57 million people. "Because of their size, modest assets and financial reserves, and higher percentages of Medicare patients, small and rural hospitals disproportionately rely on government payments" (n.p.). There is a shortage of providers in rural areas, and small rural hospitals often experience unique financial circumstances due to location and costs to improve hospital facilities.

REFERENCES

American Hospital Association. (2017). *Rural hospitals: A community's anchor.* Retrieved from https://www.aha.org/infographics/2016-02-08-rural-hospitals-communitys-anchor

Garfield, R., & Damico, A. (2017, November 1). *The coverage gap: Uninsured poor adults in states that do not expand Medicaid* (Kaiser Family Foundation Issue Brief). Retrieved from https://www.kff.org/uninsured/issue-brief/the-coverage-gap -uninsured-poor-adults-in-states-that-do-not-expand-medicaid

DISABILITY

STORIES FROM THE PROFESSION

Dr. Kristie Holmes, MSW, Los Angeles, CA

My professional career began near the end of my bachelor's degree program at California Polytechnic State University in San Luis Obispo. What was different about that university was that you had to do a senior thesis, unlike most bachelor-degree programs, which included data collection and writing up your findings. I didn't understand back then how important "studies" were. There were the things I saw in *Cosmopolitan* magazine or *Marie Claire* condensed down into something like a blog level of mass consumption reading, right? Since I was in a sorority, I was internally curious about how many women got raped at fraternity parties. The year was 1996 and Kristin Smart had disappeared from the Cal Poly campus that May. There were other strange things going on regarding campus rape, but we usually just heard about them in whispered corners. We also had rules like "don't leave a sister alone (at a party with males)."

Just like with many other things that you don't know much about until you either know somebody or it happens to you personally, only after speaking with victims did I start to truly care and focus on the issue. I volunteered for the rape crisis center and I believe that's when I got my foot in the door to advocacy. We would take night shifts in a seemingly sleepy little college town and get the most excruciating calls late at night. We'd sit with victims while the authorities used rape kits to gather evidence, and we'd listen to stupid questions about how much the young women had to drink or what they were wearing.

I've learned to help others advocate for themselves through other issues that aren't necessarily as personally violating as sexual assault but can also be traumatizing. I have had my own house burned down, experienced damage from a tornado, and most recently spent some time on a mental health deployment with the Red Cross after a hurricane. After you've had to deal with insurance companies and the runaround, the traumatizing avoidance and excuses as to why they don't want to cover catastrophic damage personally, of course you're more likely to understand in order to help those who are also going through a similar issue. Advocacy in one area can be applied to another.

In 2016 when dropping my kids off at school, I had the thing happen that nobody thinks is ever going to happen to them. I had all three kids in the car; baby number three was a surprise and he was happy as a clam in his car seat while we were dropping off the older two in the carpool lane at school. My arms started freezing up and going in odd directions and I ended up calling 911 not having a clue what was happening to me (which happened to be actively dying from two aortic dissections). The dispatcher was trying to talk me down from a panic attack and was asking how I'd been feeling since my husband left town. I explained that I was a social worker and I was pretty dang sure that this was not a panic attack. It was a very easy morning and for once there was no yelling to grab your shoes, get your bags, or hurry change the baby's diaper to get out the door. Until that moment I was a healthy woman who had just recently had a baby, and my only hospital stays were related to childbirth. I wasn't one of those people who "ran up those insurance bills." It was hard to get me into a doctor; I didn't even have a regular doctor. Most of the time I would go to urgent care if there was something amiss or I had a UTI regardless of the insurance that I had, and I've been fortunate to have great insurance through my employer most of my career. Honestly, I wouldn't know the difference had I not. That's kind of the point – you don't know until it happens to you and you can only care in theory about things like health care or heart damage, because it will never happen to you. It's rare to learn from others, taking other people's stories to heart, and that's usually because you know them well or their story is close to you while you have some connection to their experience in real time.

One of the powerful positive effects of social media and blogging has been to raise awareness of the things that you never think will happen to you or why things like advance directives are important. If I had written about it before I went to the intensive care unit (ICU) for 2 months, no one would have listened. But when I wrote and posted from the cardiac ICU with a photo of what an advance directive looked like, it made a huge impact. It's the power of personal storytelling *from you*. Friends, family, and acquaintances felt like they were experiencing what happened to me in real time as the updates came in. This was something that was happening to someone that at one point in time they knew, was their friend or even a distant cousin. It's similar to when a mass shooting is happening and you are following it in real time as victims are livestreaming it versus waking up the next morning and seeing a story headline of another shooting. Those reading desperate texts or tweets going out while bullets are flying everywhere in real time have personally invested in an issue they personally don't want to experience again, even once removed.

Anyway, back to me. My hospital billing for that first year was $14 million. That's not something anyone can save up for, exchange their home for, or even trade in their very cute children for. Kidding. The likelihood that it's going to happen to you is pretty much zero, but the outliers are somebody. That someone happened to be me. Humans with disabilities generally *are* outliers. My disability isn't something you can see from the outside – I still look pretty much the same and if you ask most people, a year later I act pretty much the same. But the truth is there's basically a yard sale inside of my chest: five stents, an internal defibrillator (ICD), and two clips holding my mitral valve together. I've been injected with stem cells and had another cath lab procedure to insert another stent, but [the surgeons] changed their mind once they got in. I was on the 1A UNOS transplant list. I was injected with enough radioactive dye to kill me. My ejection fraction is low. This just means that I have heart failure and not enough blood pumps around in my body so I get more tired than most people more quickly. It's imperative that I exercise every day, but not too much, and not lift too much because I could trigger another incident and die. I take a whole lot of medication, which of course affects how I feel, especially when there are so many per day. But mostly, I'm adjusting.

The downside is people think you're the same. And when you say "no," the same follow-ups are pursued. They don't come right out and say it but "you look fine" or perhaps more honestly, "I need you to be fine." I don't have problems with other humans avoiding eye contact with me since you can't really see my disability. If they ask to see scars (I have some good ones), I get the looks of pity, and the subject changes. I empathize with those who get this more frequently; I know how it felt when I was in the hospital and I had countless wires and tubes coming out of my neck, back, and urethra connected to a roomful of machines with my urine sitting out for everyone to see.

I can walk 2 to 3 miles on a flat surface without much problem. But if you make me stand in line or stand up in church, or stand anywhere without doing much for only a couple of minutes, I feel like I'm going to pass out. But it's hard to explain to people how I have to keep my blood moving. Thankfully my frequent flyer airline does understand this and helps out with seating so that I can move more frequently. But sometimes I feel embarrassed, or that I'm asking for special treatment by calling the disability line—even saying anything at all. There's definitely some shame attached. I'm new at this so I suspect this will change as I age or move toward transplant.

It's kind of the way you feel advocacy-wise for children who have to announce in the lunch line that they're on the free meal program because they're poor. They really don't want to have anything to do with that, but they are hungry.

Disability advocacy is relatively a new project for me. I'm seeing things from a new perspective as you can't necessarily "see" – even in cases where there are obvious needs (like a wheelchair ramp). Mostly, we miss the mark by far. Hurdles are dependent on outside factors like terrain (hills), the forecast, and whether or not someone with a disability has children with them. For instance, if I'm parking somewhere in a large parking lot in Los Angeles and I have to walk to an event, it will make a big difference whether or not it's uphill and whether or not I have children with me (specifically), plus whether or not I have a toddler with me and if he or she needs to be carried, and whether it's 67 degrees or 103 degrees out. A handicapped placard just doesn't cover all of that.

My first experience with attempting to get assistive services was at Universal Studios, Hollywood on a hot day. I felt strange waiting in the customer service line along with many others who were doing the same thing. I felt skeptical of those around me (no doubt they felt similarly about me with my able-bodied appearance). Clearly, the people at the desk hear reasons all day for trying to get a shortcut in line at a busy amusement park. I didn't like feeling like I was one of "those people" – it made me stutter a bit at the front of the line trying to explain what was "wrong" with me that needed assisted services. It felt a bit ridiculous to say that I had a heart condition and whatever is wrong with me makes it difficult to stand in line (especially holding a baby) in a way that may make me pass out because my circulation is wonky. But that I'm okay mostly walking around an amusement park for much of the day as long as it's not too hot, or on a hill because moving means circulation and that means oxygen and *not* passing out. Never mind the point that I was clearly crazy for taking three small kids to Universal Studios on my own.

I've found the most effective means of explanation is pulling down my shirt and revealing the keloid scar and raised area, which clearly shows a defibrillator on my left side top of chest. I then show my right side, which I'm told looks "like a bear got you," which is the scarring from my second heart pump. This makes them type quickly. I prefer this to long-winded explanations. But later, I feel weird about having done it in order to avoid the raised eyebrows and skepticism in order to get out of there and on with my day as quickly as possible.

It would be helpful for advocates to work with hospital staff and disability offices to ensure they are on the same page regarding diagnosis and disability terminology. This would help ensure that those who may not have a visible disability can still receive proper treatment without feeling like they have to explain or defend themselves. For instance, I did not have a card that I could carry and show which listed all of the symptoms and issues rather than having to ramble on about them in front of complete strangers in non-confidential settings.

I've tried showing my three Transportation Security Administration (TSA) device cards (for my stents, mitral clips, and defibrillator), but those behind the desk don't want to look; they want you to explain. The "Blue Book" for disability should be used as a way to override these medical information–giving scenarios in a public place to protect citizens from misuse of their confidential information (Social Security Administration, 2017).

I've had positive experiences with a major airline that I have frequent flier status with. However, I still have to repeat my issues with every single booking. Disability status can change, but it could be easily confirmed in each booking online without having to make an additional phone call and wait for ages to speak to a customer service agent, starting from scratch. At the least, it should be abbreviated in subsequent bookings (reconfirming a condition or any changes). It seems to be something that could be incorporated in the TSA process for security to avoid creating more hardship in travel for those who already have increased difficulty in doing what those without disability do. There could be designated renewal dates for temporary disability or a permanent designation available.

On that note, TSA generally fails with what I've experienced so far. Standing for long periods of time without walking around causes problems for me. There is a clear sign at airport screening areas for those with implanted medical devices to announce themselves (and not go through the screening machines) and it's worse for females (longer wait times), because there are fewer female agents employed to do a pat-down. So, a female with an implanted medical device (usually cardiac) is left standing for long periods of time, waiting for a female agent to pat her down in airport screening.

JOB DESCRIPTIONS FROM THE FIELD OF DISABILITY ADVOCACY

Legislative Liaison – Commission for Deaf and Hard of Hearing, Arizona

Education and Experience: No degree requirements posted on job posting

Salary: $36,814.34–$65,827.63

Job source: www.hr.az.gov

Responsibilities:

- Providing outreach and education as directed to the legislature on agency programs, funding sources and agency strategic goals

- Writing proposals for funding to enhance program services

- Assisting program staff in understanding the kinds and forms of information needed to support the agency legislative goals; assists the agency in working toward program effectiveness

- Attending legislative hearings, preparing legislative alerts

- Representing the agency by attending special interest group forums/meetings

- Writing and assisting in the writing of agency position papers

- Representing the commission on various committees and boards as directed

- Educating the public regarding services for persons who are hard of hearing, deaf, deaf-blind, including communication methods, accessibility, legal rights, assistive technology, consumer self-advocacy, consumer action and providing advocacy in a variety of settings for the improvement of the quality of services for populations impacted by communication barriers

Legislative Affairs Director – Wounded Warrior Project

Location: Washington, D.C.

Salary: not listed in job posting

Job source: www.woundedwarriorproject.org

Education and Experience:

- Bachelor's degree required; law or master's degree preferred

- Five (5) years of legislative, advocacy and policy experience required preferably in a government or non-profit setting

- Two (2) years management experience preferred

Summary: The Wounded Warrior Project (WWP) Legislative Affairs Director will report directly to the Senior Vice President (SVP) of Government and Community Relations and will oversee the day-to-day legislative and advocacy operations, which may include supervision of the legislative affairs team and prioritization process, as well as planning, executing, and ensuring the effectiveness of WWP's high priority legislative and policy initiatives. This position will serve to amplify the work of WWP in the National Capital Region by bolstering relationships with members of Congress and like-minded non-profits and for-profit organizations, enhancing organizational awareness, and identifying new and timely opportunities to communicate the impact of WWP programs and services.

Responsibilities:

- Assist the SVP of Government and Community Relations to develop a comprehensive plan for engaging the legislative branch in WWP legislative and policy priorities.

- Support SVP of Government and Community Relations to vet, foster, maintain, and improve relationships with federal and local lawmakers and their staffs to further WWP's effectiveness and collective impact; and further inform key stakeholders of WWP's programming, partnerships, legislative and policy work.

- Lead and develop the legislative affairs team, which may include coaching, mentoring and managing of teammates.

- Design and manage a process through which WWP can adopt policy positions, fostering buy-in from internal stakeholders.

- Support SVP of Government and Community Relations as subject matter expert on WWP legislative priorities and positions;

provide recommendations regarding policy based on in-depth research and analysis.

- Execute Hill engagements, working groups, roundtables, and other meetings at the national and grassroots levels.

- For high priority policy initiatives, develop and execute strong, well-designed advocacy campaigns at the federal and state levels that are specifically tailored to the particular issue to maximize success. Campaigns may seek legislative/regulatory changes, cultural shifts within VA or other agencies, or guidance/policy shifts.

- Work closely with Government and Community Relations team, including Communications Director, Government and Community Relations to ensure that campaigns are properly coordinated among WWP teams.

- Work closely with Director of Government and Community Relations to ensure coordinated and consistent articulation of WWP's brand and policy positions.

- Lead cross-organizational project management for advocacy initiatives.

- Ensure internal and external stakeholders, including WWP staff, are informed about initiatives.

- Forge relationships and strategic collaborations with external groups and influencers including government officials, lobbyists, fundraising professionals, and non-profit stakeholders.

- Effectively deploy and manage localized external resources to effectively represent WWP advocacy priorities.

- Provide support to SVP of Government and Community Relations to ensure he/she is effectively positioned to advocate on WWP priorities in external forums.

- Represent WWP whenever necessary at key events, meetings, discussions, hearings, conferences, or on the Hill as directed by the SVP of Government and Community Relations.

ADVOCACY FOR DISABILITY: POLICY EXAMPLES

It is critical to remember that when advocating for individuals who experience disability, many assumptions are made by lawmakers about what those disabilities look like. As social workers we know that disabilities can sometimes be invisible to the naked eye. Social Security Income (SSI) and Social Security Disability Insurance (SSDI) provide support to working-age individuals with disabilities. According to a brief published by the Center for Studying Disability Policy and Mathematica Policy Research (Livermore & Bardos, 2016), 20% of SSI and SSDI beneficiaries are parents. These parents experience poverty at high rates as compared to other beneficiaries.

Consider this: Baby boomers are just getting to the age where SSI and SSDI benefits are critical to their financial survival. Proposed cuts slash the budget another 4%, adding up to 16% in budget cuts since 2010 (Romig, 2017). Congress is *slashing* budgets at exactly the time they should be increasing funding. For more information about Social Security policies, visit https://www.govtrack.us/congress/committees/SSFI/02.

REFERENCES

Livermore, G., & Bardos, M. (2016). *Characteristics of SSI and SSDI beneficiaries who are parents* (DRC Data Brief No. 2016-02). Washington, DC: Center for Studying Disability Policy & Princeton, NJ: Mathematica Policy Research. Retrieved from https://www.mathematica-mpr.com/our-publications-and-findings/publications/characteristics-of-ssi-and-ssdi-beneficiaries-who-are-parents-drc-data-brief

Romig, K. (2017, October 6). *More cuts to Social Security Administration funding would further degrade service.* Washington, DC: Center on Budget and Policy Priorities. Retrieved from https://www.cbpp.org/research/social-security/more-cuts-to-social-security-administration-funding-would-further-degrade

Social Security Administration. (2017). *Disability evaluation under Social Security – Listing of impairments – Adult listings.* Retrieved from https://www.ssa.gov/disability/professionals/bluebook/AdultListings.htm

MENTAL HEALTH

STORIES FROM THE PROFESSION

Dr. Angela Henderson, MSW, Washington, D.C.

My interest in physical environments stems back to my life experiences in North Carolina. There are so many happy memories that come to mind when I think of my home state. One thing is for sure: It is easy to fall in love with North Carolina's weather and breathtaking scenery. There's nothing like staring up at the beautifully painted North Carolina sky or taking scenic routes to look at miles and miles of lush green vegetation. There's a majestic form of happiness and tranquility that comes over me when I think about North Carolina's gorgeous physical environments.

Throughout the years, as I traveled back and forth through North Carolina and various other states, I started noticing vast differences in the layout, structure, and composition of cities and towns. Then one day out of the blue, driving along a highway, I started to think to myself, what gives? When I traveled to certain areas within a city or town, there were flourishing trees, colorful parks, dazzling homes and buildings, sculptures, spacious sidewalks, and, in some places, bountiful waterways. But in other areas of the same city or town, there was an absence or scarcity of vegetation, massive clouds of chemicals floating into the sky from factories and company plants, land barren with sand, dreary and dark-colored buildings and homes, vacant lots, landfills, and broken or small sidewalks. Even though the neighborhoods and communities with dreary physical environments seemed desolate in some ways, the areas were rich with the communal love, support, and culture of their residents. But I still could not believe my eyes. It was hard for me to forget the vast differences in physical environments of cities and towns on the basis of zip codes.

I started to make additional startling observations by zip code when comparing the differences between neighborhood and community environments. I noticed that a large portion of the communities and neighborhoods within the cities and towns with depleted physical environmental features were located in areas frequently populated by low-income populations and/or people of color. Various feelings started to bubble to the surface for me. My stomach dropped and I started to feel a mixture of anger, sadness, and a sense of urgency. I took some time to process my feelings, and I began to think about how I could best address the disparities that existed between different physical environments within cities and towns across the United States. I decided to dig deeper and find out how these drastic physical environmental differences impacted the mood and mental health of populations with low income and/or people of color.

Through research, I discovered that my observations were valid. Our physical environments, both natural and built, can have positive and harmful effects on our mental health. Extensive research has shown that there is a long history of hazardous physical environmental features being disproportionately located in neighborhoods and communities with low-income populations and people of color. The disproportionate numbers of people of color and low-income populations exposed to hazardous physical environmental elements located within neighborhoods and communities is alarming. Why on earth would we place hazardous materials around any human being, let alone any living organism? Numerous research studies have shown linkages between physical environmental features that include air toxins (atmospheric ozone, particulate matter, sulfur dioxide, and nitrogen dioxide), metals and chemicals (oil, lead, and pesticides), noise, and natural disasters and mental health conditions. Attention-deficit/hyperactivity disorder, stress, anxiety, posttraumatic stress disorder (PTSD), depression, and brain impairment (impairment to cognitive development and functioning) are some of the mental health conditions that can result from exposure to hazardous physical environmental features in cities and towns.

This is where the "rubber meets the road." I decided that I wanted to make a difference in the lives of people at risk of or subjected to exposure of harmful elements within their physical environments. I figured out that the best way for me to fight for the rights of Americans and promote environmental justice would be to generate research and advocate for policies to alleviate and reduce exposure to hazardous physical environmental elements. I feel so empowered when I conduct research studies. I also wanted to provide people with an opportunity to learn about the restorative impact the physical environment can have on their lives. There is extensive research detailing the beneficial effects of physical environmental factors on the mental health of various populations of people. Research involving psychological restoration has shown how exposure to clean waterways (streams, lakes, rivers, and oceans), built environments (trails, parks, sidewalks, houses and apartments, buildings, and sculptures), and vegetation (trees, forests, flowers and plants) can positively affect people's mood and alleviate the presence of mental health conditions (stress, fatigue, anxiety, and depression).

Research studies provide me with a deeper and clearer understanding of how the hazardous and beneficial environmental elements truly affect the clients and communities that we serve as social workers throughout the United States and the world. One particular research study I conducted found correlations between noise and poor air quality and PTSD symptoms among African American youth residing in urban neighborhood environments in the northeastern region of the United States. The findings from the study have far-reaching ramifications when it comes to understanding how physical environmental elements function not only as health stressors but also as mental health stressors in the lives of the youth living in urban environments. The data from the study provided the youth and their families and communities with a deeper understanding of how noise and poor air quality can create PTSD symptomology (i.e., effects on perceptions, mood, and thinking patterns, emotions, memory, behavior, lifestyle, and relationships). With all research studies that I conduct, I also like to search for resiliency factors that protect people from harmful elements that exist within their physical environment.

Within the same research study, I found out that the youth and their perception of the physical environment in which they live can drastically impact the presence of PTSD symptomology. For example, my research study uncovered the fact that Afrocentric ethnic identity functioned as a protective factor in the relationship between noise and poor air quality in relation to PTSD symptoms in African American youth. Afrocentric ethnic identity is grounded in traditional, African-centered cultural values that highly affirm cultivating and fostering positive relationships with people, nature, and the universe throughout life. The youth in the research study who embraced life from an Afrocentric perspective felt empowered and emboldened to make changes and improve their neighborhood environments, thereby protecting them against developing symptoms of PTSD. The research study provided me with an opportunity to inform residents about the harmful elements and protective factors that affected their mental health.

I gained valuable life lessons as a result of conducting the research study. Every human being should feel empowered to speak out against the harmful effects of toxins, chemicals, and destructive natural disasters that devastate their neighborhoods and communities. Residents should never live in fear of retaliation because they decide to speak out against environmental injustice and discriminatory practices affecting their well-being and life span. It is critically important for social workers to continue to be at the forefront to eradicate human beings' exposure to toxins within the environment that damage their mental health. As social workers, we must continue to assume leadership positions in local, state, and federal legislative offices and advocacy organizations in order to shape environmental policies that protect the mental health and well-being of all Americans. I will continue to advocate for local and state legislative officials and Congress to pass laws that eradicate and restrict the production of hazardous environmental toxins within the cities and towns that we live in. It is critical for the United States to track the detrimental progression of climate change on our ecological system.

In classroom settings, I have the opportunity to connect with upcoming generations of social work leaders to discuss strategies and solutions involving pressing environmental traumatic events like the Flint (Michigan) water crisis, Hurricane Harvey, Hurricane Maria, the Sierra Leone mudslides, the Gulf of Mexico oil spill, and the northern California fires. The students gain critical insight on the work environmental social workers like myself are taking part in to assist clients and communities. I work with the students to help them achieve a deeper understanding of environmental justice and its connection with protecting the rights and freedom of all human beings. Through the work that I do, I am able to reinforce the fact that every person deserves the right to live in a healthy environment not impeded by inequality and institutional discrimination. It is imperative to collaborate across professions with scientists, doctors, nurses, entertainers, and lawyers to address environmental justice issues plaguing our society and world. Every human being deserves the right to know how harmful environmental features affect their lives without interference from people who believe monetary profit and individualism outweigh the healthy progression of all Americans' mental health.

JOB DESCRIPTIONS FROM THE FIELD OF MENTAL HEALTH

Government Relations – Texas Psychological Association

Salary: 50,000–55,000 per year

Location: Texas

Education and Experience: Bachelor's Degree plus 3 years legislative activity

- Coordinate and promote TPA's legislative agenda

- Establish and maintain communication between state legislators, their staff, and the TPA executive committee

- Provide a strong and credible voice for TPA with members of the Texas Legislature

- Advise TPA's legislature committee and BOT in establishing legislative priorities, advise PAC regarding TPA's legislative contributions campaign, advise the BOT and executive director in developing legislative days and action alerts, consult with grassroots coordinator and attend grassroots committee meetings at grassroots coordinator's request

- Serve as a member of TPA's legislative committee and attend those committee meetings/calls as well as BOT meetings and the annual TPA convention, to provide legislative updates to membership

Public Policy Specialist – Mental Health and Intellectual Disabilities

Education and Experience: Bachelor's degree in public policy, political science, disability studies, education, social service or other related field of study plus 7 years of experience

Salary: not listed

Location: Texas

Job source: https://www.disabilityrightstx.org

Job Description: Train and assist case handlers while collaborating with team members to identify opportunities for policy advocacy. The public policy specialist will also conduct policy research, write policy reports, and provide internal and external training. This individual will work closely with stakeholders to disseminate pertinent information using work groups, advisory boards, task forces and committees. Will also assist with annual grant reports and work in conjunction with local, state, and national organizations, agencies, legislatures, and public officials to protect and advocate for the rights of individuals with disabilities.

Director of Policy and Legislative Affairs – California Council of Community Behavioral Health Agencies

Education and Experience: Bachelor's degree required and at least 4 years of increasing levels of legislative and public policy responsibility required. Experience addressing policy and legislation in all areas of behavioral health including mental health and substance use disorder services and programs.

Job source: www.indeed.com

Location: Sacramento, California

Salary: $120,000–$140,000 annually

Responsibilities: The Director of Policy and Legislative Affairs is responsible for utilizing the state legislative and budget processes to advance the advocacy agenda of CCCBHA and its member agencies.

Overview: Provide legislative, policy, and advocacy services as established annually by the Executive Director and CCCBHA Board of Directors serving as CCCBHA's legislative and public policy advocate on state behavioral health bills, budget items, and other priority issues affecting nonprofit behavioral health contractors. Activities include testifying on said items/issues as necessary, providing legislation analysis, coordinating appearances by CCCBHA representatives at legislative and regulatory hearings, participating and providing input to policy committees addressing mental health issues, providing materials regarding designated legislative matters to CCCBHA and its members affected by legislation, assisting CCCBHA and its members in the solution of problems created by legislation; managing a master calendar that tracks hearings, testimony, and other items of importance to the CCCBHA's legislative program; and providing regular and periodic updates to CCCBHA members on legislative, budget and policy developments, and general matters of interest with respect to the behavioral health field including mental health and substance use disorders.

Director of Public Policy – National Alliance on Mental Illness (NAMI)

Location: Arlington, Virginia

Salary: not listed in job posting

Job source: www.nami.org

Education and Experience:

- 10+ years' experience preferred, but will consider less if experienced in mental health financing, coverage and/or quality

- Advanced degree required or bachelor's degree and equivalent experience

- Excellent written and verbal communication skills

- Minimum 4 years' supervisory experience

- Extensive knowledge of mental health policy and financing

- Knowledge of state and federal legislative processes

- Ability to work independently and take initiative

- Proven ability to effectively manage budgets and program goals and outcomes

- Ability to respond quickly and effectively to time-sensitive issues

- Strong project management and leadership skills

- Exceptional organizational skills and attention to detail

- Proficiency with Microsoft Office suite

- Ability to work collaboratively within a team environment and across teams

- Flexibility and ability to respond to and prioritize competing demands

- Demonstrated experience in forging collaborative and effective relationships

Essential Duties and Responsibilities:

- Leads research and analysis of federal and state legislation and regulations to inform policy positions and priorities, especially Medicaid financing and coverage

- Leads strategy for and manages key multi-faceted initiatives, including alternative payment models for evidence-based mental health interventions, Medicaid and non-Medicaid state funding, mental health coverage and parity

- Develops strong relationships and works collaboratively with stakeholders, including leading national partner organizations, coalitions, think tanks and federal agencies

- Leads analysis of and makes recommendations on state Medicaid waivers

- Develops effective strategies and tactics in response to time-sensitive policy issues and opportunities

- Leads advocacy initiative on quality measures for mental health care

- Leads analysis and strategy regarding mental health coverage, including parity requirements and access to mental health services and supports

- Develops policy briefs, reports, blogs, op-eds and other policy content

- Serves as an expert consultant to media and elected officials on mental health policy issues

- Represents NAMI and presents on policy issues at state, regional and national meetings

- Facilitates effective inter-team and cross-team collaboration

- Manages budgets for policy initiatives and reports to national director on program deliverables

- Assists with funding proposals and grant reports, including meeting with funders

- Leads and manages direct reports, including facilitating their professional growth and development

Housing Program Manager, St. Martin's Hope Works – Albuquerque, NM

Job source: www.indeed.com

Job Summary

Hope Works is looking for an experienced Housing Program Manager with HUD and Housing First knowledge and experience. Responsible for SMHW housing funds (leases, continuum of care [including Welcome Home], supportive housing); oversight of SMHW housing programs under the direction of the behavioral health director.

Duties will include:

- Act as LLA lead for state program.

- Maintain monthly demographics.

- Act as liaison to Housing Manager and Community Support Workers who provide Comprehensive Community Support Services to Housing clients as well as to the SMHC Director of Behavioral Health Services, who serves as the Agency HMIS Administrator and oversees SMHW's provision of Medication Management services.

- Maintain client files in a manner matching or exceeding HUD expectations.

- Attend HMIS training and oversee quality of HMIS data for all Housing Programs using HMIS.

- Produce monthly reports in form of monthly City draw-downs.

- Perform HUD inspections on rental units.

- Train staff to conduct HUD inspections.

- Conduct Voucher briefings and train Housing Staff to conduct such briefings.

- Maintain record of and perform annual HUD re-inspections.

- Produce Quarterly and Annual reports for the City of ABQ, MFA, HUD, and any contact as requested.

- Undergo annual site visits.

- Work with CFO and Dir. of BH Services on financial matters related to grants, including CoC funds.

- Develop annual budget for the department and manage the department budget throughout the year.

- Send various notices of violation.

- Manage/oversee intake of all new Housing clients ensuring they meet eligibility requirements.

- Work in partnership with agencies who conduct VI-SPDAT.

- Work in partnership with partnering agencies to obtain required housing documentation.

- Perform annual training regarding Housing Programs for St. Martin's Hope Work Staff.

- Attend various meetings with associated agencies.

- Participate and prepare for audit compliance.

- Update and develop Standard Operating Procedures as needed and as requested from supervising staff.

Supervision:

- Responsible for supervising and overseeing the functions of the Housing Department Staff.

- Daily scheduling and supervision.

- Set expectations of job requirements.

- Ensure compliance with paperwork requirements.

Other Duties and Responsibilities:

- Act as liaison to other agencies concerning housing issues.

- Research low-income housing opportunities for clients.

- Attend various conferences and training focused on housing issues.

- Carry out all duties in a manner that is consistent with SMHW mission and philosophy including Housing First and policies.

Education, Experience and Licensure Requirements:

- Bachelor's degree required.

- Must be able to speak in public, providing workshops and various presentations.

- Experience working with HUD, and other Housing programs, including Housing First.

- Detail oriented with ability to handle multiple deadlines.

- Supervisory/administrative experience.

- At least 1 year experience with SDMI population/homeless adults.

- Prefer NAHP certification.

Job Type: Full-time
Job Location: Albuquerque, NM
Required education: Bachelor's
Required experience: Working with SDMI population: 2 years
Required license or certification: NAHP

Life Skills Coach (FT), The Price Center – Newton, MA

Salary: $14–$16 an hour

Job source: www.indeed.com

Who We Are
The Price Center, founded in 1977, is a non-profit human service organization in Newton Highlands. We are a values based and team focused organization offering residential services, employment supports and day habilitation programs. Our mission is to support and enhance the lives of individuals by encouraging personal growth and active participation in the community, and respecting individual preferences and diversity. For more information on The Price Center, please go to our website at: http://www.thepricecenter.org

Summary
The Life Skills Coach position in the Specialized Supports Day Services program is structured with a small (1:1, 1:2, 1:3) staff/participant ratio focused on skill acquisition and experiential learning through community exploration. Our participants may be on the autism spectrum, non-verbal or just need a more specialized approach to learning. We are seeking a dynamic, personable, energetic and responsible person to work in this growing program.

Duties and Responsibilities
Under the supervision of the clinical management team, the Life Skills Coach is responsible for the direct care of individuals in the day program, including the use of Applied Behavior Analysis (ABA) principles and techniques.

- Work with individuals on a variety of tasks throughout their day (tasks may include: social skills, communication and language, academics, vocational skills, community behavior and activities of daily living).

- Utilize strategies to teach social and communication skills to allow program participants to succeed in the community.

- Consistently collect accurate data for individual programs, daily living skills, vocational skills and behavior (frequency, antecedent-behavior-consequence, duration, etc.) in a timely manner.

- Have a thorough knowledge and competent implementation of all program participant programs and behavior management guidelines implemented in the program and in the community.

- Ensure all participants' safety and implement all safety procedures.

- Record and compile all necessary behavioral and educational research data accurately.

Qualifications

- Applicants must be bright, energetic individuals with a strong desire to work with individuals with developmental disabilities and autism, and experience in or an interest in being trained in the principles of applied behavior analysis.

- Minimum of 1-2 years of experience working with individuals with developmental disabilities and autism preferred.

- Candidates who have completed an associate's degree given preference; minimum of high school degree and two years related experience in a care giving or educational environment; hospital, school, day program, etc.

- Knowledge and understanding of principles of normalization, behavior management and human rights.

- Excellent written and oral communication skills so that writing of required documents is clear and articulate.

- Strong ability to work in a team style environment.

- Obtain/maintain necessary certifications (CPR, First Aid and Crisis Intervention Training).

- Ability to lift and support body weight of any program individual with the assistance of another employee.

- Valid Driver's License, good driving record and a willingness to use personal and agency vehicle in the course of employment.

Hours & Salary:

– Full-Time, 40 hours per week

– $14–$16 per hour

Our comprehensive and generous benefit package includes:

- Competitive health insurance (employer pays 85% of premium)

- Dental insurance

- Employer paid Life and Long Term Disability

- 403(b) matching retirement plan

- Tuition reimbursement and tuition remission programs

- Generous Vacation, Sick, and Personal Time Benefits

- 12 Paid Holidays

- $1,000 Employee Referral Bonus with no annual cap!

ADVOCACY FOR MENTAL HEALTH: POLICY EXAMPLES

The Water Infrastructure Improvements for the Nation (WIIN) Act of 2016 gave $100 million to the city of Flint, Michigan, to assist in fixing the compromised water system in the city. Despite this funding, the people in Flint still do not have clean water and have not had clean water since 2014. The lead contamination alone will have long-term, irreversible neurological consequences on the city's children (Lurie, 2016). The mental health implications for all of the residents of Flint are disastrous. This is an excellent policy opportunity for social justice intervention.

Meanwhile, in Mississippi, House Bill 886 (failed) and Senate Bill 2567 (failed), the Mississippi Health Agency Reorganization Act of 2017, would change the way the public mental health system is structured and operated. These bills would place the Mississippi Department of Mental Health (along with the Mississippi Department of Health and Mississippi Department of Rehabilitation Services) under the control of the governor and places the Board of Mental Health in an advisory role (Barry, 2017). Placing the Department of Mental Health under the purview of the governor means that mental health services would fall under the control of an elected official with no formal education in providing mental health services throughout the State of Mississippi.

REFERENCES

Barry, J. R. (2017, January 29). Reorganization bill detrimental to mental health. *Clarion Ledger*. Retrieved from https://www.clarionledger.com/story/opinion/columnists/2017/01/29/reorganization-bill-detrimental-mental-health/97209840

Lurie, J. (2016, January 21). Meet the mom who helped expose Flint's toxic water nightmare. *Mother Jones*. Retrieved from https://www.motherjones.com/politics/2016/01/mother-exposed-flint-lead-contamination-water-crisis

SUBSTANCE ABUSE

STORIES FROM THE PROFESSION

Tasha Perdue Forquer, MSW, Toledo, Ohio

I still remember her laugh and the way she liked to joke about my driving. Sarah[1] was my first interaction with someone diagnosed with comorbid mental health and substance misuse disorders. She helped to form me as a social worker, a field that was not in my original career plans. My initial goal throughout high school was to become an investigator. I majored in criminal justice for my undergrad program, with an ultimate dream to work for the Federal Bureau of Investigation (FBI). During my coursework I became drawn to structural theories for crime and deviance. While my classmates discussed the need to increase penalties and the benefits to a tough-on-crime approach, I discussed the need to consider the surrounding context and understand economic, structural, and educational barriers associated with crimes within communities. An experience as a summer camp counselor with inner-city youth was my first exposure to social work. It was this experience that made me consider social work as an alternative career option. My senior honor's thesis, a documentary about females experiencing homelessness and service provision within local shelters, solidified my decision to pursue social work, rather than law enforcement, as a career.

My first position after graduating from my undergraduate program was as a community mental health case manager. I had a Medicaid-funded caseload of 40 individuals with an array of diagnoses and differing treatment needs.

---

[1]Name changed

It was a difficult job with high demands of certain billable hours of client contact every month and paperwork deadlines requiring overtime, despite a lack of overtime pay. The position was stressful and the pay was minimal. After interacting with case managers who had been working there for 20 years, it was obvious that burnout was a possibility. Despite the negative aspects, I loved my interactions with those I had the privilege of serving as a case manager. I always knew that it would be a temporary position, as I did not have the qualifications to move into more management or leadership roles. Although I knew the position was temporary, I was determined to learn as much as I could during this time period.

Sarah was transferred to my caseload within the first few months. As I interacted with and learned from her, she provided a foundation for me as a beginning social worker and helped to shape perspectives that I hold today. Although Sarah presented challenges to someone new to the field, I appreciated identifying and working toward her strengths. She was diagnosed with bipolar disorder and cocaine use disorder. Her cocaine use disorder escalated in intensity and began to affect her mental and physical health. After becoming heartbroken by the burn marks on her fingers caused by the crack pipe, and her worsening cough due to her prolonged crack cocaine use, I found what appeared to be a perfect treatment setting and helped her to get enrolled – only to face utter disappointment when she left after 2 weeks. I dealt with negative comments from my coworkers. "You can't trust people who are addicted. They are manipulative. We just can't help them." Despite all of the negative comments from social work coworkers and all of the self-doubt, I persisted and adapted, eventually learning to put her needs first. She did not want treatment. I wanted treatment for her and she acquiesced, as she felt it would ease my concerns. It was during this time I learned the important lesson of meeting individuals where they are and respecting the right to self-determination. I was not aware of harm reduction as a concept at the time, but in retrospect I took this type of approach in my future interactions to meet Sarah's goals while planning for her safety.

As the years passed, I became frustrated at structural barriers that impacted insurance coverage for medication, the fact that insurance payment time periods dictated when individuals were released from psychiatric units even if they could have benefited from additional time, and the overall stigma directed toward those on my caseload when we were in the community together. I also felt powerless in my role at times. The tipping point happened after I became aware that one individual on my caseload was obtaining multiple prescriptions from different pharmacies. She mentioned paying one doctor in cash and divulged that she was receiving prescriptions for multiple opioids, including Vicodin, Percocet, and OxyContin. I approached her psychiatrist with my concerns over the potential for interaction with her psych medications. The psychiatrist informed me that the individual in question suffered from back pain and needed the prescriptions. Despite my elaboration on the suspect nature of how the individual obtained the prescription pain pills, the psychiatrist effectively shut down any other dialogue on the topic. This was in 2008, during the early stages of the opioid epidemic, and the issue had not reached the level of national dialogue. After being informed that my concerns were baseless, I became discouraged at the lack of communication between mental and physical health providers. Further, I felt a power imbalance due to my age and inexperience, and I believed that questioning the psychiatrist would be futile. It was at this point that I realized that I needed to pursue my master's degree in social work (MSW), so that I could address changes on a macro level.

During my MSW program internship, I became involved in community organizing and policy advocacy work related to human trafficking, with a focus on domestic minor sex trafficking (DMST). At this time Ohio was one of the last states that did not designate human trafficking as a stand-alone felony. On the federal level, the Trafficking Victims Protection Act established that anyone under the age of 18 was a victim without the need for proof of force, fraud, or coercion. Although the federal legislation could be used to prosecute traffickers, the state felony distinction was needed to address gaps in prosecution and allow the trafficker to face maximum penalties. At this time youth were still being labeled as juvenile prostitutes by law enforcement and social service providers, and the language had not yet shifted to DMST victims. Service providers characterized the DMST victims as "bad kids" and focused on the secondary behaviors related to trafficking, such as runaway behavior. Victims often faced injustice in court proceedings. For example, a 13-year-old victim was charged with prostitution whereas the adult male who purchased services received no charges. It was evident that additional policy was needed, but the state legislators would need to be convinced. One of my major intern projects was contributing to a state report that was used by legislators to make human trafficking a felony. I also became active on the community level and assisted in founding a local coalition uniting multiple stakeholders to establish policies and procedures related to trafficking while increasing awareness and education. The coalition had a diverse membership ranging from community members, health and social service providers, researchers, FBI agents, nuns, and even empowered sex workers. I served as secretary for the coalition, before later being elected to cochair the coalition.

Following my graduation I pieced together multiple micro- and macro-level grant-funded positions, including research assistant, regional epidemiologist, women's group leader, and visiting lecturer. On the mezzo level I continued to volunteer my time with the trafficking coalition, the annual international human trafficking conference, and provided free trainings around the state. I also became active with state and federal policy makers, later receiving a certification of recognition for my community work related to trafficking from the county commissioners and special recognition from the Ohio House of Representatives, 45th House District of Ohio. One of the highlights of my macro policy advocacy efforts during this time was providing testimony to the Ohio Legislature in support of policy targeting the demand side of human trafficking. Human trafficking has three components: supply (victims), distribution (traffickers), and demand (customers). Policy initiatives have started to focus more on demand, so that customers are held accountable, whereas in the past customers often testified against the trafficker to escape penalties, despite their participation in sexual victimization. As I listened to the primarily male lawmakers discuss questions over whether increased protections for victims might increase false accusations, I became more aware of the need for empowered female voices in political advocacy to stand against the status quo.

Although my mezzo and macro work began with a focus on human trafficking, my position as regional epidemiologist began to attract my intellectual interest. Through this position I contracted with the state of Ohio conducting research related to drug trends. During this time the prescription opioid and heroin epidemic was beginning to take hold throughout the country, and Ohio was especially impacted. As I conducted focus groups with those in substance abuse treatment, treatment providers, and law enforcement, the same themes arose. Individuals were prescribed large amounts of prescription pain medications and would find themselves physically dependent on the pills. Legislation was introduced to curb prescribing patterns and individuals began transitioning to heroin, which was cheaper and more potent than the pills.

Seeing the epidemic grow and overdose rates steadily increasing, I knew that I wanted to contribute more, and that change through research and policy advocacy was where I belonged. I decided to pursue a PhD in social work with a focus on opiate use transitions and trajectories. When I first started my program, I had practically no knowledge of harm reduction. My home state had one harm reduction center when I left for my PhD program, and although I had heard of syringe exchange programs, I was not educated on how they operated. During my first and second year in my program, I engaged in volunteer work at a harm reduction center to learn more about this public health philosophy. Harm reduction takes an approach of meeting clients where they are, and focuses on minimizing adverse consequences associated with drug use such as overdose, HIV and hepatitis C transmission, and incarceration. Services can include syringe exchange programs, naloxone overdose prevention training, wound care, psychosocial groups, and supervised consumption facilities. As I worked with the staff and clients of the harm reduction center, I thought back to my first experiences working with Sarah. I remember how I tried to encourage her to pursue an abstinence-based approach to treatment and met with failure. It was only when I began to meet her where she was, and employ a "safety first" planning approach, that we made strides in meeting her treatment goals.

I am now an advocate for harm reduction approaches, with a particular focus on supervised consumption facilities. Although my participation in community organizing and policy advocacy is currently limited due to my dissertation obligations, I am finding ways to support and advocate for harm reduction approaches. My current papers and projects have a harm reduction bent to them, and I include some discussion over harm reduction in my presentations at conferences. I discuss harm reduction with my former colleagues engaged in micro-level work and provide materials so that they can become further educated. I retained my connections to community organizers in Ohio and provided suggestions and materials as they implemented a syringe exchange program in my former town. Although I am currently not as engaged as I would like to be, I have been able to bring my micro-level harm reduction volunteer work experience and my new macro-level skills to assist in protocol development. I feel fortunate to continue to find fulfillment in merging the different levels of social work practice.

Despite the ability for the different levels of social work to complement each other, I have noticed a divide between micro and macro practice within my different social work roles. As a micro social worker, I have experienced the impact of policies and protocols created without the knowledge of how those receiving services, and the social workers providing services, would be impacted. One policy change in particular stands out. While I was a case manager, the agency transitioned to treatment planning based on diagnosis. This severely limited the ability for the individual to be active in his or her own treatment goals. The diagnosis-based treatment planning only lasted a few months, but resentment toward the change lingered. Conversely, as a macro social worker involved in policy advocacy, I have also been on the other side. I advocated for policy changes that did not consider how the agency would be affected. When human trafficking legislation was passed in Ohio, the Children's Services Agency was mandated to provide care for victims. This caused a change in their internal policy, as the original responsibility was to provide care for individuals abused by family members or guardians. Under the new legislation, the agency would need to care for the DMST victims, even if the family or guardian was not involved in the trafficking. The new mandate to Children's Services was unfunded, so the agency would need to increase its scope of care, without an increase in funding. Unfortunately, in our zealous advocacy for the policy change, we had not considered the impact of the mandate, and the implementation process would have been much smoother had the front-line staff been involved in policy conversations.

Moving into a role within academia, I have also noticed the divide in the classroom among students. Micro-oriented students have initially expressed less interest in the policy and research classes that I have taught, while macro-oriented students often neglect to incorporate an understanding of the social worker in the field and experiences of clients. As I continue to grow as a social worker, and into a role of training other social workers, the need to blend micro, mezzo, and macro together to make effective change becomes more evident. This is one reason I am drawn to qualitative research. Although quantitative analysis provides an understanding of prevalence and gives policy makers impetus for change, the numbers are meaningless without an understanding of the lived experience. For me, qualitative research is the best practice, as it allows me to engage with the population I am passionate about, while involving them in developing the most effective approaches for prevention and intervention.

My journey from micro- to mezzo- to macro-level work has not been a linear process, and I currently do not define myself as a micro, mezzo, or macro social worker. Rather, I see myself operating within a continuum, where I can use research and policy advocacy to make changes, but one in which I need to remain aware of what is happening on the micro and mezzo level. I am a multi-level social worker blending all of the practice levels in order to effect the most change. Without such integration the individuals, agencies, communities and systems of care will face a disservice from a profession created to make a difference.

JOB DESCRIPTIONS FROM THE FIELD OF SUBSTANCE ABUSE ADVOCACY

Substance Abuse, Legislative Advocacy Coordinator, Baltimore Harm Reduction Coordinator

Job source: www.indeed.com

Salary: No salary listed in job posting

Education and Experience:

- A successful candidate for this position will be highly organized, detail oriented, and comfortable working independently. They must be skilled at collaboration with a variety of stakeholders and collective decision-making. Additionally, they must be outgoing and feel comfortable convening a coalition of diverse individuals (including people who have been targeted by the war on drugs and anti-sex work policy, law enforcement, family advocates, treatment providers, etc.) about potentially sensitive issues (drug use, overdose, sex work, etc.).

- Candidates should have knowledge of and commitment to harm reduction and racial justice as well as demonstrated knowledge of the Maryland legislative process.

Responsibilities:

- Identify and contact new coalition members, focusing on groups and individuals directly impacted by the war on drugs and anti-sex worker policies.

- Provide leadership to the statewide coalition, including scheduling regular calls, planning agendas, and documenting meeting action items.

- Interpret, analyze, and draft statutory language and legislation based on coalition consensus.

- Track progress of relevant legislation in the MD General Assembly, and communicate this progress and advocacy opportunities with coalition members.

- Coordinate with the BRIDGES Coalition (https://www.facebook.com/Bridges-Coalition-1760625273964186/about) and other stakeholders to develop harm reduction advocacy/educational strategy (including materials) for legislators and other advocates.

- Work collaboratively with and assist in providing a meaningful learning experience to a Peer Advocacy Intern.

- Coordinate an advocacy training in Baltimore for BHRC members.

- Coordinate an advocacy event in Annapolis with coalition members.

- Participate in regular meetings with supervisor (Executive Director) and other project leadership (BHRC Advisory Board and BHRC Policy Committee Chair).

- Prepare reports to fulfill grant requirements.

Substance Abuse Prevention Specialist

Job source: http://www.d19csb.com

Location: Petersburg, Virginia

Salary: $32,000–$45,000

Education: Bachelor's degree in Human Services Field and considerable experience working with families and children, teaching and/or public speaking and experience in the substance abuse field

Responsibilities:

- Delivery and promotion of prevention services (school and community based) for nine localities in District 19 Community Services Board

- Implementation of prevention strategies that include needs assessment and recommendation for prevention strategies

- Program development

- Strong presentation skills

- Working with children and families in a community based setting to reduce prevalence of substance abuse and related problems based upon sound research based principles and processes

Project Coordinator/Teen Advocacy Coalition – Willapa Behavioral Health

Location: Raymond, Washington

Education: Bachelor's degree in related field

Salary: No salary information provided

Responsibilities:

- Manage a Drug Free Community initiative devoted to help youth succeed. This role is the liaison between the Teen Advocacy Coalition and three local high school districts, community organizations and volunteers.

- Must be passionate about substance abuse prevention, supportive mental health services and willing to encourage teen leadership and community involvement.

Program Administrator, Community Services Board

Job source: www.governmentjobs.com

Salary: $47,822.70–$77,977.98

Location: Norfolk, Virginia

Education: Bachelor's degree plus 3 years' experience in program management or related field. Two years' experience in treatment of persons with substance abuse and mental health issues in a correctional setting with 2 years supervisory experience.

Responsibilities:

- Work closely with local hospital emergency rooms, emergency services, and crisis stabilization staff to provide client perspective on a comprehensive assessment to determine individualized treatment preferences.

- Assist peer recovery specialist in helping clients in developing recovery plan by identifying client's strengths, goals, and steps toward recovery to include needed supports.

- Assist peer recovery specialists as they help clients with general problem solving and development of skills in obtaining services and supports through coaching toward an increased sense of responsibility.

- Ensure that clients learn about available community resources and that peer recovery specialists advocate for services on behalf of clients as needed.

- Support peer recovery specialists as they act as liaisons between clients and other service providers to ensure that client preferences expressed in recovery plans are included in individual service plans.

- Ensure that peer recover specialists maintain accurate data collection and documentation consistent with agency guidelines, grant requirements, and licensure standards.

- Collaborate with multiple programs as part of a treatment team, community services providers and significant others as necessary.

- Facilitate staff meetings, case review meetings and staff training activities as required.

- Utilize SAMSHSA's crisis prevention and other recovery oriented peer support programs.

- Encourage peer recovery specialists as they help clients develop skills and strategies to prevent relapse of substance addiction and possible mental health symptoms, reconnecting them with their recovery goals.

Drug and Alcohol Prevention Coordinator, State of Maryland

Job source: www.jobaps.com/MD

An Alcohol and Other Drug Abuse Prevention Coordinator is the full performance level of work in a single person program, assessing, designing, coordinating and implementing alcohol and drug abuse prevention programs within a local health department. Employees in this class do not have supervisory responsibilities.

Employees receive general supervision from a higher-level healthcare administrator in the Department of Health and Mental Hygiene's headquarters office.

Positions in this classification are evaluated using the classification job evaluation methodology. The use of this method involves comparing the assigned duties and responsibilities of a position to the job criteria found in the Nature of Work and Examples of Work sections of the class specification.

The Alcohol and Other Drug Abuse Prevention Specialist is differentiated from the Alcohol and Other Drug Abuse Prevention Coordinator in that the Alcohol and Other Drug Abuse Prevention Specialist performs the full range of staff duties under general supervision in a multi-person program. The Alcohol and Other Drug Abuse Prevention Coordinator is responsible for administering a single person program, performing the full range of duties under general supervision of a headquarters healthcare administrator. The Alcohol and Other Drug Abuse Prevention Coordinator is differentiated from the Alcohol and Other Drug Abuse Prevention Supervisor in that the Alcohol and Other Drug Abuse Prevention Supervisor has full supervisory responsibility for Alcohol and Other Drug Abuse Prevention Specialists. The Alcohol and Other Drug Abuse Prevention Coordinator does not supervise but works a single person program.

Examples of Work:

- Monitors data collection to identify the problem areas specific to the community in order to develop, in the assigned local health department, addictions prevention plans and increase community awareness;

- Develops, coordinates and implements prevention educational programs and alternative youth activities to decrease and prevent drug and alcohol involvement and related risk behavior;

- Maintains and distributes alcohol and drug abuse prevention educational materials;

- Assists community groups, other agencies and organizations in developing, organizing and conducting programs to prevent and resolve conditions and problems related to alcohol and drug abuse;

- Plans, organizes and conducts training for staff of other State and local agencies, schools, local businesses, industries and community groups involved in alcohol and drug abuse programs;

- Prepares and maintains reports, records and documents pertaining to funding sources, program evaluation and reference information on chemical dependency;

- Develops and implements the alcohol and drug abuse prevention policies and procedures;

- Prepares grant proposals for addictions prevention projects;

- Evaluates the alcohol and drug abuse prevention program activities of the local health department to determine effectiveness and efficiency;

- Confers with the local health officers and program directors to recommend remedial or corrective actions to prevent alcohol and drug abuse problems;

- Develops and maintains a wide variety of alcohol and drug abuse educational services for use by program directors, school personnel, private and public organizations and the general public;

- Performs administrative functions related to the overall direction of the addictions prevention components within the local health departments;

- Performs other related duties.

Knowledge, Skills and Abilities:

- Knowledge of disease concepts of alcoholism and drug abuse dependency;

- Knowledge of principles and practices involved in the development and implementation of alcohol and drug abuse education and intervention programs;

- Ability to stimulate community action in the development of effective alcohol and drug prevention programs;

- Ability to compose promotional and educational literature relating to alcohol and drug abuse prevention;

- Ability to provide consultation in the areas of occupational alcoholism and/or drug abuse for employee assistance programs;

- Ability to effectively present topics on substance abuse;

- Ability to establish and maintain working relationships with other professionals and agencies.

Minimum Qualifications:

- Education: Possession of a bachelor's degree from an accredited college or university with thirty credits in behavioral science, health services, human services or education.

- Experience: Two years of experience in counseling alcohol or drug dependent clients; in providing therapeutic education services to alcohol or drug dependent persons and their families; or in directing school or community health education.

Notes:

1. Sixty credit hours from an accredited college or university to include 18 credit hours in the behavioral sciences, health services, human services or education and an additional two years of experience as specified above may be substituted for the required education.

2. Additional experience as specified above may be substituted for the required education on a year-for-year basis.

3. Graduate level education in behavioral sciences, health services, human services or education may be substituted for the required experience on a year-for-year basis.

4. Candidates may substitute U.S. Armed Forces military service experience as a commissioned officer in Drug and Alcohol Counseling or Health Care Administration classifications or Mental/Behavioral Health and Drug and Alcohol Counseling or Health Services Administration specialty codes in the health related field of work on a year-for-year basis for the required education.

Licenses, Registrations and Certifications:
Employees in this classification may be assigned duties which require the operation of a motor vehicle. Employees assigned such duties will be required to possess a motor vehicle operator's license valid in the State of Maryland.

Rehabilitation Specialist – Alpine Special Treatment Center, Alpine, CA

Job source: www.indeed.com

Salary: $14.55–$19.05 an hour

Mission: Alpine Special Treatment Center Inc.'s (ASTCI) mission is to provide an environment where adults with mental illness and co-occurring disorders transition from acute crisis to stabilization. Clients' safety and well-being is maintained while encouraging and promoting individuals' highest level of independence through an integrated, individualized and comprehensive therapeutic program. ASTCI provides a welcoming environment and goal oriented program that gives the mentally disabled and dually diagnosed individual the tools necessary to transition back into the community while maintaining a more independent lifestyle.

Facility Information: ASTCI is a secure, 113-bed mental health rehabilitation facility located 28 miles east of downtown San Diego. ASTCI has been providing services to the County of San Diego for 40 years. Our facility is CARF accredited, and recognized for excellence in providing treatment to clients, most of whom are conserved due to severe disability. We are proud to announce that Alpine Special Treatment Center has been selected as the 24-hour Program of the Year by the Mental Health Recognition Committee of San Diego. This is validation of our excellent program and dedication to our clients. ASTCI is open 365 days a year, 24 hours a day. You can learn more about Alpine Special Treatment Center Inc. by visiting: http://astci.com.

Job Description: Alpine Special Treatment Center, Inc. is currently seeking dynamic, caring, Masters-level clinicians to work closely with clients in a direct-care, team-based environment within an inpatient treatment setting. In addition, Alpine Special Treatment Center, Inc. is seeking individuals with an interest in leadership, and the ability to manage and provide support to a team of direct care staff during their shift. The position is fast-paced, team oriented and provides the opportunity for clinicians to gain experience in the treatment of clients struggling with severe and persistent mental illness while also gaining skills in leadership, compliance, and therapeutic interventions.

Duties: The Psychosocial Rehabilitation Specialist (PSRS) position works closely with clients in a direct-care, team-based environment on the secure dual-diagnosis units, to provide daily care to clients residing at the facility. Initially, entry level Psychosocial Rehabilitation Specialists learn the facility's policies and model of care and complete duties in line with the facility policies and model of care. Duties include the facilitation of groups and activities that support the psychosocial rehabilitation model, monitoring and observation of clients, activity of daily living support, documentation, crisis prevention/intervention, contraband searches, inventory checks, admission and discharge preparation with clients, and medication/meal monitoring. This position is offered under direct supervision at all times. Additionally, this position must demonstrate strong professionalism skills, dependability and adherence to HIPAA, client rights, safety and other pertinent regulations associated with client care. Advancement on the career ladder to Psychosocial Rehabilitation Specialists level II, III or IV is possible with demonstrated competency against the benchmarks outlined in the job description with related increases in the pay rate. The ability to make a difference in clients' lives, increase knowledge of mental illness, enhance leadership, interpersonal and communication skills is limitless in this fast-paced and supportive environment.

Work Schedule(s): Full-Time (40 hrs per week)

Working Days: Mon, Tue, Wed, Thu, Fri, Sat, Sun; 1st Shift 7:00 am to 3:30 pm; 2nd Shift 10:00 am to 6:30 pm; 3rd Shift 3:00 pm to 11:30 pm

NOTE: Shifts may vary depending on client care needs, days off may not include standard weekend days or holidays. Flexibility in scheduling is favored.

Salary/Benefits: Competitive hourly rates commensurate with experience and the Psychosocial Rehabilitation Specialist role, from $14.55–$19.05/hour.

Night and weekend shift differentials are available, along with holiday premium pay. Comprehensive training to include crisis de-escalation certification (provided by the facility within first 90 days of employment). Company-paid health insurance within 60 days includes: Medical, Dental, Vision, Life/AD&D, and Long-Term Disability.

Paid time off (PTO), 401(k) retirement program. All Psychosocial Rehabilitation Specialists are eligible for ASTCI's quarterly incentive bonus program and additional career advancement opportunities during his/her tenure at ASTCI.

Key Requirements:

- Must pass pre-employment physical examination
- Must be proficient in written and spoken English
- Designated drug testing required
- Able to successfully pass a criminal background investigation (DOJ/FBI)
- Verification of educational credentials through a certified transcript
- Crisis intervention experience
- Team player
- Excellent communication and observation skills

Qualifications Education or Training: B.A. or B.S. in Psychology, Social Work, Counseling, or related field (or graduating within 3 months)

Experience: 2 years' experience working in a mental health setting may be substituted for the educational requirement.

Certification: Current/Valid CPR certification (AHA AED/BLS/Healthcare Provider)

Physical Requirements: This position requires walking, standing, and sitting for long periods of time. Incumbent will be climbing stairs, lifting up to 50 pounds, use dexterity of the hand and wrist and arm strength to perform various reoccurring tasks. As a component of the crisis prevention/intervention duties, the position may require a "hands on" component of the job associated with working with individuals that at times may present as aggressive or threatening due to their mental health symptoms.

Preferred Qualifications: Successful Psychosocial Rehabilitation Specialist practical experience in a psychiatric and/or substance abuse treatment setting is highly preferred.

Job Type: Full-time

ADVOCACY FOR SUBSTANCE ABUSE: POLICY EXAMPLES

An interesting thing happens when you type "substance abuse policy" into the Google search engine. All of a sudden you are directed away from advocacy websites and news articles and instead you encounter examples of "policies" that businesses can use to enforce drug-free workplace policies. Addiction is a complicated issue. In the United States we have legal and illegal drugs that are often used to the point of addiction. On the federal level, the Substance Abuse and Mental Health Services Administration (SAMHSA) administers funding to states in order to address addiction.

The Overdose Prevention and Patient Safety Act (H.R. 3545, Rep. Tim Murphy [R-Pennsylvania]) would place all substance use disorder (SUD) patient records under the much looser protections of the Health Insurance Portability and Accountability Act (HIPAA) (Knopf, 2017). This would eliminate the confidentiality laws that lead to many people seeking treatment.

REFERENCE

Knopf, A. (2017, October 2). Patient confidentiality campaign launched in 42 CFR Part 2 battle. *Alcoholism and Drug Abuse Weekly, 29*(38), 1–5.

AGING

STORIES FROM THE PROFESSION

Dr. Troy Christian Anderson, MSW, Salt Lake City, UT

Rita Fowler was born on December 16, 1900. The world had just entered into a new century, and there were many cultural and societal changes that were occurring at this time. What Rita did not know at the time was that average life expectancy for people born in the year 1900 was only 47. She also had no idea that in her lifetime she would live through and experience World War I, the influenza pandemic of 1918, which ended the lives of 50 million individuals worldwide, the Great Depression, World War II, and the advent of automobile and airplane travel. Rita also did not know that she would live to reach 83 years old, that she would bury three husbands, and that she would see her grandchildren and great-grandchildren become adults.

My grandmother Rita was a force to be reckon with. She stood approximately foot 4'9" but had a larger-than-life personality. When I was in elementary school, my mother returned to college to complete her master's and doctoral degrees. During that time, I spent afternoons with my grandmother and looking back, there were many experiences that shaped my interest in working with older adults.

Rita was fascinated with family history and spent hours chronicling past generations of our family. As each of her grandchildren reached 8 years old, she would present them with a book of family history that included many photos of interesting ancestors. I recall a specific photo of a distinguished, middle-aged gentleman with a handlebar mustache, who was a territorial marshal prior to Utah's statehood. My grandmother would share stories about visiting her relatives and how it would take several days to travel the 40 to 60 miles between homes. These rich stories influenced my interest in knowing about and working with elders.

Another memorable event was when my grandmother met her third husband, Alex. I have a vivid image of this couple, who were then in their 70s and 80s, sitting in a loveseat in my grandmother's bungalow home in Salt Lake City. He was dressed in a suit and she was in a fine dress. They were announcing to the family their plans to be wed. I recall thinking that they seemed a bit old to be getting married.

In the final chapter of my grandmother's life, we began to witness changes in her health and cognitive status. After the death of her third husband, my grandmother continued to live independently, but we began to see changes in her memory and decision making. She would purchase Christmas gifts for various family members, all of which were not very well suited for the recipient. I recall one teenage cousin getting a toddler dress. We would discreetly give the gift to someone of the appropriate size and age. We eventually found out that my grandmother was suffering from vascular dementia. An interesting note is that I am currently working in a highly specialized dementia diagnostic center and routinely see individuals with vascular dementia, Alzheimer's disease, and related dementias.

My grandmother died just as I was entering college. My mother was a social worker, and her career also deeply shaped my own career path. I studied psychology as an undergrad and decided to shift to do my graduate degree in social work. I graduated with my master's degree in social work (MSW) in 1989 and began my career working with children, adolescents, and families. I found my clinical work to be interesting and invigorating; however, I never lost sight of the fact that I had a particular interest in working with older adults. Approximately five years into my career, I began working full time in the emergency department as a mental health crisis worker. In this very demanding setting, it was my responsibility to complete mental health evaluations and to play a role on the trauma team. In this role, I worked with families of individuals seen for acute trauma, life-threatening illness, and unexpected death. During the 15 years in this clinical setting, I enjoyed my work on the trauma team most of all. I felt it an honor and a privilege to participate and support families in these very difficult moments of extreme crisis. In working with death and its aftermath, I was reintroduced to my interest in working with older adults and with end-of-life issues. After 15 years of working in this highly intense setting, I decided that a career change was needed. As I explored alternative job opportunities, I had the good fortune to meet with our new Division Chair of Geriatric Medicine. I inquired about positions in geriatric outpatient settings and he replied at the time that there were no current opportunities. He did, however, alert me to a newly founded dementia specialty clinic that was being established at the University of Utah. I applied for this position and, with no clinical experience working with individuals with dementia, I was selected. As I began to develop a greater understanding of the various forms of dementia, I became fascinated with what happens when damage occurs in the brain and how that impacts function.

A year after I began this position, I decided that I would return to school to seek additional education. I first enrolled in a master's degree program in gerontology. This training helped me develop additional foundational understanding and enhanced my expertise in working with older adults. One year after I embarked on this journey, I decided to apply for the PhD program in social work. The programs coupled well together and I was able to utilize my newly gained knowledge in aging as well as my developing expertise in dementia to craft my dissertation research. I completed research on the integration of social work and health education into the diagnostic process in a dementia specialty clinic. The focus of this model is to engage the individual with dementia and the person's primary care partner and family in developing a clear understanding of the disease process, to be preventatively aware of the changes that occur within the disease, and have a proactive approach to managing care across the disease span. To complete the story, once I finished my PhD, I was fortunate to find a split academic appointment between the College of Social Work, where I teach courses related to health and aging, and an appointment within the School of Medicine, where I continue to engage in clinical work as well as doing aging-related research.

As I began my more intensive teaching and research roles, I became increasingly aware of the varied ways in which advocacy is critical in addressing the pressing issues faced by older adults today. As stated previously, our society has experienced a drastic shift in demographics over a 100-year period. Whereas life expectancy for people born in 1900 was about 47 years, people born in 2000 have an additional 30 years of life expectancy. This change is due, in part, to addressing acute illnesses that lead to untimely and unexpected deaths. Treating commonly occurring infectious diseases is a big part of this medical advancement. With the advancement of life expectancy, we are now encountering a variety of ethical, clinical, and psychosocial issues. We are now faced with addressing whether quality of life is extended as we seek to extend quantity of life. We have transitioned into a health care model of managing multiple chronic conditions, and we have the potential to continue to extend life expectancy over the coming decades. With this life extension, we are seeing individuals who are living in increasingly frail functional states with increased risk for exploitation, financial devastation, and lack of adequate care opportunities. In the remainder of this chapter I will address what I see as leading examples of the need for social work and other helping professions to be engaged in direct advocacy to improve quality of life and care for older adults.

I will first examine policies that impact all older adults and then will address specialized populations that need special advocacy interventions. One of the most glaring policy shortcomings that I have encountered in my clinical and research practice is the nearly complete lack of financial supports to pay for the cost of long-term care. Many older adults and even practicing clinicians do not recognize the fact that Medicare, the universal payer of health care for those over 65, does not contribute to the cost of home-based and facility care supports for people with chronic conditions. Over the previous century, we have transitioned our medical model from an acute care model to a management of chronic health care needs. Medicare's payment model is basically shaped around an acute care payment approach in a chronic care health care world. Medicare does not pay for home-based personal care supports, assisted living, or skilled nursing facilities outside of the realm of rehabilitation. The onus for payment and provision of care for older adults is placed directly on the individual and his or her family.

In researching this issue further, I found that there are government-run approaches, in developed countries, that have established universal care payment models that address the cost of long-term care for their elders. Japan is an example of a country that has directly addressed this issue and has come up with a working model. In Japan individuals at age 40 begin to pay into a fund for long-term care services when they reach retirement age. This funding is similar to the way in which Medicare and Social Security are funded in our country. As individuals in Japan age into the retirement window, they will have various care support options made available to them. These options can range from direct personal care in the home setting, adult day center care, and residential care, which mirrors our assisted living and skilled nursing facility care.

In the development of the Affordable Care Act, an attempt was made to integrate a similar approach into our Medicare program. This was called the Class Act. This act heightened the awareness of this void and need for programs to support care. This act, however, did not survive the multiple iterations that eventually were passed into law. As of now, we have had no additional conversations on how to address this urgent issue, and each decade we delay will continue to change the problem's size and scope. From an advocacy perspective, this is a very difficult policy to address. The cost involved in attempting to create a universal plan for addressing the cost of long-term care is astronomic.

The next policy arena that I encountered in my clinical work was the need to address the complex medical and care needs of individuals with Alzheimer's disease and related dementias. In 2011 Congress passed the National Alzheimer's Project Act. This act established a national plan for how to address the priorities for research, medical treatment, and care of individuals with Alzheimer's disease–related dementias. Building off of this work, a committed group of individuals, led by my boss and the director of the Cognitive Disorder Clinic at the University of Utah, Dr. Norman Foster, crafted and sought legislative support for Utah's State Plan for Alzheimer's disease. This action plan was created to establish state-specific priorities in addressing the changing needs of patients and families. Even with this victory, challenges remain. In spite of the fact that we have established this plan, many of the objectives have lacked financial support to proceed toward fruition. We have continued to work with our legislative leaders to obtain consistent financial support to ensure these critical needs are addressed.

Finally, I have had the opportunity to work with two vulnerable segments of the older adult population that have critical advocacy needs. The first group is the LGBTQ older adult population. Entering into the world where home-based care supports and facility-based care commonly occur, many older gay and lesbian individuals and couples find that they do not feel safe welcoming direct care workers into their homes and do not feel welcome in entering into assisted-living centers where dated policies and prejudice create hostile and unwelcoming environments. Many choose to forgo seeking help based on fears of being treated unjustly. Working with two colleagues, we are crafting trainings to educate direct care workers and administrators on how to create a culture of acceptance.

The second group that I am beginning to work with is the population of incarcerated older adults. After decades of increasingly harsh sentencing policies, prison administrators and staff are being required to address increasingly complex medical needs of aging inmates. I am beginning a new research project that targets evaluating the medical needs of older inmates and the environmental and practitioner limitations of supplying this complex medical care.

Over the past 100 years, we have seen a drastic demographic shift in our country and in the world. Older adults are the fastest growing age group across the life span and are also the group with the most complicated medical, social, and financial needs. Our efforts to address ethical issues, medical care, and policies have not kept pace with the complexities at hand. I have highlighted a number of examples of this expanding problem. Unfortunately, in the United States, the current approach to addressing these complex needs seems to be to do nothing but wait and see. Direct, vocal, and consistent advocacy is required to change our current direction. A final lesson that I learned from my grandmother is that change requires dogged persistence. Happily, dogged persistence seems to be a trait that I have inherited and that I utilize routinely in my work.

JOB DESCRIPTIONS FROM THE FIELD OF AGING ADVOCACY

Manager, National and Community Partnerships – National Council on Aging

Education and Experience: Bachelor's degree

Location: United States, exact location not listed

Salary: Salary not included in job posting

Job source: www.ncoa.org

Responsibilities:

- Have a direct influence on improving the health and economic security of 10 million older adults by 2020.

- Form new partnerships to connect with NCOA's economic security and health aging programs and services.

- Connect with faith based, community based, regional and national organizations that have contact with and represent diverse and hard to reach senior populations.

- Build relationships, attend conferences, conduct meetings and assess partner needs to assist and support them.

- Create a strong presence for NCOA so that more seniors are reached.

- Promote and encourage culturally competent communication and education on public benefit programs with diverse and hard to reach senior populations.

- Collaborate with NCOA's economic security, health, aging, public policy and advocacy teams to ensure organizational goals are considered (increasing access to benefits like Medicaid, Medicare, SNAP,

LIHEAP, access to evidence based programs like Chronic Disease Self-Management and Falls Prevention, etc.)

- Establish and maintain positive relationships with stakeholders at a variety of organizations to assist in achieving program goals.

- Provide expertise about local, national and industry trends and best practices for expanding access to public benefits for target populations.

- Work with Federal Partners Work Group and other partners of the Center for Benefits Access.

- Disseminate information and knowledge to consumers, practitioners and partners through websites, newsletters, presentations, publications and monthly webinars.

- Present at conferences and other events.

- Assist with developing funding proposals.

- Assist in writing grant reports.

- Contribute to current body of literature that generates and spreads new knowledge to analyze current and future practices.

- Assist with developing cost effective outreach strategies.

Community Coordinator – New York City Department for the Aging

Job source: www.nyc.gov

Salary: $50,362–$78,177

Location: New York

Education and Experience: Baccalaureate degree and 2 years of experience in community work or community centered activities in a related area.

Responsibilities:

- Assist Deputy Commissioner of External Affairs on special projects, including working with the Age-Friendly Commission and its sub-committees.

- Provide support to the Director of Government Affairs, including tracking legislation, working with advocacy groups, preparing testimony and other support as necessary.

- Help prepare for annual Borough Budget Consultations and Public Hearings on DFTA's Annual Plan Summary.

- Assist with preparing talking points and speeches for the agency as needed.

- Attend community meetings by the Interagency Council on Aging, Community Boards, elected officials and others.

- Prepare briefings for the Commissioner and Deputy Commissioner.

- Assist with preparation and coordination of the DFTA Senior Advisory Council.

- Prepare regular reports on behalf of the bureau to the Mayor's office and Commissioner.

- Liaise with other city agencies and represent DFTA at interagency meetings on various initiatives, e.g., Vision Zero, LGBTQ, ECT.

Social Program Manager – Baltimore City Health Department

Salary: Depends on Qualifications

Location: Baltimore, Maryland

Job source: www.governmentjobs.com

Experience and Education: Bachelor's degree in Public Health or Human Services and 3 to 5 years of experience in program management and supervision.

- Must have interest in serving the public, specifically older adults and adults with disabilities.

- Must be able to work with members or city government, for profit and nonprofit organizations.

- Familiarity with Older American Act funded programs.

Responsibilities:

- Report to the Division Chief of Advocacy Services and collaborate with other units within the division and agency for operations and programmatic concerns, compliance and opportunities.

- Collaborate with other team members in the operation of the MAP programs for Baltimore City, which includes acting as a liaison between the department and relevant community groups and associations.

- Establish program goals, which includes planning, coordinating and approving activities that are consistent with state mandates for assistance services. This may include outreach, activities, education, resource linkage and triage.

- Assist in budget planning for program operations and facilitate the reconciliation of invoices and services within the program.

- Communicate with other departments, the public government and private agencies.

- Assist in facilitation of the contract processes with multiple vendors, programs and employees.

- Supervise and evaluate program staff.

Social Worker – Skilled Nursing Facility, Scottsdale, Arizona

Job source: www.ensigngroup.net

Job Summary

The medical social worker is responsible for the implementation of standards of care for medical social work services.

- Assesses the psychosocial status of patients related to the patient's illness and environment and communicates findings to the registered nurse.

- Carries out social evaluations and plans intervention based on evaluation findings.

- Maintains clinical records on all patients referred to social work.

- Provides information and referral services for organization patients and families/caregivers regarding practical and environmental needs.

- Provides information to patients or families/caregivers and community agencies.

- Serves as liaison between patients or families/caregivers and community agencies.

- Maintains collaborative relationships with organization personnel to support patient care.

- Maintains and develops contracts with public and private agencies as resources for patient and organization personnel.

- Participates in the development of the total plan of care and case conferences as required.

- Assists physician and other team members in understanding significant social and emotional factors related to health problems.

- Participates in discharge planning.

- Other duties as delegated by the Director of Nursing/Supervisor.

The above statements are only meant to be a representative summary of the major duties and responsibilities performed by the employee of this job. The employee may be requested to perform job-related tasks other than those stated in this description.

Job Requirements
(Education, Experience, Knowledge, Skills & Abilities)

- Graduate of a bachelor's program in social work accredited by the Council on Social Work Education.

- Minimum of one year's experience in health care.

- Experience in a home health care preferred.

- Demonstrates good verbal and written communication, and organization skills.

- Possesses and maintains current CPR certification.

- Must be a licensed driver with an automobile that is insured in accordance with state or organization requirements and is in good working order.

Gerontology Social Worker – NPG Geriatrics, Naples, Florida

Job source: www.healthcaresource.com

Job Summary
The Social Worker independently assesses, plans for and coordinates for the discharge planning needs of patients, using standards of care and policies and procedures. Assumes teaching and leadership responsibilities. Participates in departmental, unit committee and performance improvement activities. Needs minimal supervision.

Essential Duties and Responsibilities – *Other duties may be assigned.*

- Provides discharge planning, assessment and counseling services to Baker Act, Marchman Act and patients referred under the CAGE protocols.

- Assessment: Demonstrates the ability to complete a thorough assessment of a patient's anticipated discharge and psycho/social needs, as part of the hospital's discharge planning processes.

- Discharge Planning: Implements discharge plans for patients in a timely and appropriate manner, in accordance with hospital policies. Intervenes throughout a patient's hospital stay and when appropriate will present information to the patient/family with option to best utilize community resources. Continually evaluates the effectiveness of the discharge planning process and community resources.

- Resource Utilization: Demonstrates the ability to work effectively with patients, families and the treatment team to reduce the incidence of avoidable days and to lower the hospital's/unit's average length of stay. Appropriately refers to UR staff cases that need to be reviewed.

- Customer Satisfaction: Demonstrates the ability to work effectively with patients, families and the treatment team to improve customer satisfaction with the hospital's services, to include the overall and discharge planning customer satisfaction scores.

- Knowledge of Community Resources: Demonstrates the ability to maintain an excellent working knowledge of community resources, the ability to incorporate appropriate resources into a patient's discharge plan and the ability to retain a positive working relationship with outside community services.

- Clinical/Interviewing Skills: Demonstrates the ability to effectively manage an interview with a patient/family to provide crisis intervention/counseling services and to help implement an appropriate discharge plan to meet a patient's needs. Works closely with a patient/family to help them adapt to sudden life changing conditions resulting from the patient's illness.

- Collaborative Teamwork Skills: Demonstrates the leadership, teamwork, communication and interaction skills with other members of the treatment team, so as to promote and maintain a high degree of satisfaction with the department's services. Serves as a resource to staff and physicians. Participates in discharge planning meetings and clinical team meetings.

- Advance Directives: Demonstrates the knowledge base and counseling skills to effectively assist patients with advance directives and completes work on all assigned advance directive referrals in accordance with hospital policies.

Education, Experience and Qualifications

- Minimum of Bachelor's Degree in Social Work or related field

- Minimum of 2 years of experience in Social Work or an NCH Social Work Internship

ADVOCACY FOR AGING: POLICY EXAMPLES

The National Council on Aging (https://www.ncoa.org) has some wonderful resources on policies that directly impact older adults. Their public policy and action page can help you understand key pieces of legislation in the coming years.

In September 2017, Senator Susan Collins (R-ME) sponsored Senate Bill 1028 (the RAISE Family Caregivers Act), a bill to provide for the establishment and maintenance of a national family caregiving strategy and for other purposes (Brophy, 2017).

In 2017, the Trump administration's proposed budget made historic cuts to and eliminated many critical programs that help seniors and their families. For example, the budget completely eliminated funding for the Medicare State Health Insurance Assistance Program (SHIP). SHIP provides local insurance counseling to Medicare beneficiaries, their families and caregivers. The budget eliminates this program, which supports 15,000+ counselors who provide free, state-specific assistance to over 6 million beneficiaries (National Council on Aging, 2017).

With current and impending cuts to Medicare, social justice advocates who are interested in advocacy for older adults are going to very busy sorting out exactly how seniors are going to access critical programs to not only sustain their lives but thrive later in life.

REFERENCES

Brophy, B. (2017, September 27). Congress takes step to aid family caregivers. *AARP Newsletter.* Retrieved from https://www.aarp.org/politics-society/advocacy/info-2017/senate-passes-family-caregivers-act-fd.html

National Council on Aging. (2017). *Medicare State Health Insurance Assistance Program (SHIP)* (NCOA Issue Brief). Retrieved from https://www.ncoa.org/resources/ncoa-2017-issue-brief-medicare-state-health-insurance-assistance-program-ship

CRIMINAL JUSTICE

STORIES FROM THE PROFESSION

Dr. Gretchen Heidemann Whitt, MSW, Los Angeles, CA

My career as an advocate for prison reentry reform and for justice for formerly incarcerated women started shortly after I received my master's degree in social work (MSW) in 2004. These were the days when terms like *prison industrial complex* and *mass incarceration* were starting to find their way into everyday language. Activists and academics alike were beginning to spell out the myriad ways in which the tough-on-crime, three-strikes-you're-out, and war-on-drugs policies that began in the 1960s and really flourished in the 1980s and 1990s were impacting poor communities and communities of color. And the massive costs of the massive lockups were starting to be felt by local and state jurisdictions who were becoming interested in reducing prison spending. It was a time ripe for advocacy.

Let me say a little bit about myself before I go on. I am a White woman from the Midwest who has never been incarcerated. I'm from a middle-class family, and I had ample opportunities to pursue higher education. I could have chosen just about any career or profession and would have had the support and resources I needed to go for it. But I chose social work because being of service to others and investing my time and energies in correcting the wrongs that I became aware of through my education and other exposures felt more important to me than anything else. Does that make me a martyr? No. The beautiful thing is that I've never had to sacrifice myself. Any deficit in my paycheck that I may have experienced working in the nonprofit sector was more than made up for by donated Thanksgiving dinners and other similar perks.

Does it make me pollyannish? Maybe. You can decide for yourself after you read the rest of my story.

So, where were we? Right. I had just finished my MSW. I was working for an organization called the Los Angeles Coalition to End Hunger & Homelessness (LACEH&H) and I was spearheading a campaign to register homeless and very low-income people to vote in the 2004 presidential election. It was painstaking work, but we registered more than 2,000 folks and drove them in vans to polling places on election night. It was truly energizing, and I was feeling very empowered and eager to continue the work. Unfortunately, the grant supporting my position ended after the election and there were no funds for LACEH&H to keep me on. Fortunately, however, at precisely the same time, a woman by the name of Ms. Susan Burton, who served on the LACEH&H Board of Directors, received a grant from the Women's Foundation of California to conduct focus groups of formerly incarcerated women about their health concerns and the impact that prison had had on their health. Ms. Burton ran a program in South LA called A New Way of Life Reentry Project, which helped women transition from prison and jail back into the community. She communicated to my boss, Bob Ehrlenbush, at LACEH&H that she was looking for someone to come work for her to conduct the work spelled out in the Women's Foundation grant. Bob put me in touch with Susan, and I went to Watts for an interview.

Susan's office was in the garage of a small house on 91st Street. There were a couple of desks and shelves lining the walls, a conference table in the middle of the room, and lots of papers and donated items in the room. It was different than any work environment I had ever been in. There was a buzz about the place. Women were coming and going from their appointments, cooking food, watching television, and searching for jobs on the shared house computer. The phone rang frequently, and it was clear from observing Ms. Burton that she handled matters swiftly and with authority. Another woman, Dr. Marilyn Montenegro, also participated in my interview. She was a social worker who had been a mentor to Ms. Burton for many years and who supervised social work interns at the organization pro bono. I was told a bit about the project that was being funded and about the history of the organization. I was asked if I thought I could perform the work and if I was interested in the position. I said yes, and that was that! I was hired! It was short and sweet, no fluff, and I got started right away.

I loved interacting with the women. I relished in their stories, especially when we were all just sitting around the dinner table. There was no filter, no hierarchy; we were just a bunch of women talking about life and what had had happened that day. I learned so much from them and felt privileged to bear witness to their daily struggles and triumphs. I enjoyed being there so much that I set myself to the task of raising money so that I could stay onboard long-term. After my experience being let go from LACEH&H due to lack of funds, I thought there must be a way to support my salary through grants. And so, having zero experience as a grant writer, I started researching and writing proposals. Much to my surprise, we brought in enough that I was able to remain at A New Way of Life for several years until I decided I wanted to pursue a PhD.

My daily tasks quickly expanded to include everything under the sun. I was one of three staff members at A New Way of Life. In addition to Ms. Burton, there was a housing manager who cooked meals, ran errands, oversaw the chore schedule, and basically kept the two reentry homes running. Just some of the things I remember doing include taking women to AA meetings and appointments at the Social Security and Welfare offices to help advocate for their benefits, starting up a parenting group for women who were reuniting with their children, reaching out to local employers to encourage them to consider hiring women with prior convictions, and attending community meetings as the organization's representative. I also continued grant writing and became very involved in planning the organization's annual fundraising gala. I loved having my hands in the full range of micro- and macro-level activities; there was a profound and obvious connection for me between the women's past experiences, the barriers they were facing to rebuilding their lives, and the individual- and systems-level advocacy we were doing to help pave a path to success for them.

My involvement in advocacy really took off one day when Ms. Burton, after returning from a weekend-long summit of formerly incarcerated people, asked me to work on drafting an ordinance that we would bring before the LA City Council asking them to reconsider how and when people are asked about felony convictions on job applications. We called it the "Ban the Box" campaign because we wanted to get rid of that box that people must check on the very first page of a job (or housing, or student aid, or welfare, or community college) application that asks about any prior criminal record. Our experience working with the women in the reentry homes told us that "the box" discouraged many people from even attempting to apply for jobs, and, more pertinently, it gave potential employers an excuse to toss the application in the trash can without knowing the circumstances of the conviction, the extent of rehabilitation, or the unique qualifications that a person might bring to the job. We didn't want to completely eliminate a background check. Of course, it is necessary for employers to know of an applicant's criminal history, but, we argued, the applicant should have the chance to be considered alongside other applicants and their qualifications noted before consideration is given to the nexus between the job and any prior conviction.

At first, our campaign had little traction. Few city council members were willing to hear our argument; fewer still were willing to champion our cause. But we didn't give up. We shifted strategies and decided to target smaller locales. We went to the cities of Carson and Compton, where large swaths of the community had been caught up in the vast net of the drug war. Council members in these locations knew that expanding job opportunities would have a positive effect not just for individuals but for the entire community. Once we had secured some of these smaller victories, we went back to the Los Angeles City Council. With a new mayor at the helm and several new council members, our advocacy strategy worked! The City of Los Angeles passed the Fair Chance Initiative for Hiring Ordinance (FCIHO), which states, in part, that the city and its contractors "cannot inquire about an applicant's criminal history until after a conditional offer of employment has been made." (For more information, see https://bca.lacity.org/fair-chance.)

Our partners in northern California, in Boston, in Chicago, and in many other places around the country began to experience similar victories. Our movement quickly caught on, and cities, counties, states, and even private industries began adopting "Fair Chance" hiring policies. I was overcome with a sense of pride when, more than a decade later, I read the headline that former President Obama was announcing a "ban the box" regulation for hiring within the federal government (Boyer, 2016). Our message, which started with a handful of individuals in Watts and East Palo Alto had grown so strong and so loud that President Obama had heard!

My career in advocacy was a natural outgrowth of my desire to help those who had fewer opportunities and resources than I did. It wasn't enough to shuttle women to their appointments and help them, one by one, acquire employment. Those efforts were necessary. But for change to happen "upstream," we had to testify before the city council, hold press conferences, and make a lot of noise. I am grateful to have played even a small part in the "Ban the Box" campaign that eventually made its way to the White House.

JOB DESCRIPTIONS FROM THE FIELD OF CRIMINAL JUSTICE ADVOCACY

Community Engagement and Policy Advocate – ACLU of Southern California

Location: Bakersfield, California

Job source: www.indeed.com

Salary: Salary not listed on job posting

Education and Experience:

- Commitment to the cause of civil liberties and civil rights, including economic justice, voting rights, and political participation.

- Two or more years of organizing, campaigning, and advocacy experience.

- Cultural competency, including the ability to sustain inclusive and engaging spaces for all people of all races/ethnicities, genders, ages, classes and geographies.

- Outstanding interpersonal and communication skills.

- No mention of degree in job posting.

Responsibilities:

- Establish and maintain relationships with community partners, stakeholders, coalitions and ACLU members.

- Assist in identifying issues surrounding policing and immigrant rights arising in Kern County and advance the ACLU SoCal and ACLU of CA immigrants' rights and policing work as well as other ACLU agendas.

- Participate in community partner meetings and coalitions that focus on immigrants' rights and policing issues.

- Provide strategic guidance, training, and support for community members and coalition partners conducting local policy advocacy.

- Create training programs and materials on priority immigrants' rights and policing issues and conduct trainings and presentations as needed.

- Organize, lead and participate in community education events, rallies and meetings.

- Write blogs and social media content.

- Help identify and tell compelling human stories to center the experiences of communities affected by civil and human rights abuses.

- Serve as a spokesperson for the ACLU SoCal both with press and as a public speaker on policing and immigrants' rights related issues.

- Build effective grassroots and policy advocacy campaigns.

- Develop relationships and partnerships with organizational allies to advance policy objectives.

- Draft advocacy letters and recruit diverse and powerful allies to sign on to the letters.

- Develop advocacy materials such as fact sheets, toolkits, action alerts, blog posts, and social media content.

- Track national, state, and local developments relevant to policing and immigrants' rights policy objectives including legislative activity.

- Organize and attend lobbying visits with state and local officials; provide testimony to administrative agencies and governing bodies.

- Provide trainings for community members and coalition partners on how to conduct policy advocacy with decision makers.

- Activate and mobilize volunteers, ACLU members and other community partners and organizations around key actions and policy priorities.

- Occasionally research and write policy briefs.

Director of Sexual Assault – Advocacy and Prevention Services

Job source: www.indeed.com

Education and Experience: Bachelor's degree in human services field or equivalent experience in the field

Location: Streator, Illinois

Salary: not listed in job posting

Responsibilities:

- Coordinate and monitor the delivery of counseling and prevention services.

- Direct and facilitate continual program improvement.

- Build community relationships.

- Provide professional trainings.

- Serve as a liaison with the Illinois Coalition Against Sexual Assault.

- This Agency provides trauma informed services to victims of domestic and sexual violence and non-offending family members.

Policy Specialist/Sr. Policy Specialist, Criminal Justice

Location: Denver, Colorado

Salary: $4,428+/month depending on experience

Job source: www.ncsl.org

Education and Experience: Bachelor's degree plus 5 years of relevant and progressive work experience

General Description:
NCSL's Criminal Justice Program is seeking a Policy Specialist/Sr. Policy Specialist to perform quality legislative research, writing, assist with meeting planning, and handle information requests. The Policy Specialist/Sr. Policy Specialist will work on general and emerging criminal justice topics, based on the needs of the Program. This includes tracking state legislation, recognizing and analyzing criminal justice policy trends, developing web based material, preparing briefs, and making presentations to legislatures and other audiences. The individual will improve and develop new creative website documents and features that effectively inform NCSL's members, and assist with details and logistics for the Program's multitude of meetings. The successful candidate will have background/experience with criminal justice issues, understand the state legislative policy process, be a good writer and strong public speaker, and bring energy and creativity to a variety of team activities. It is expected that the position will include independent work and work as part of the Criminal Justice team, sometimes requiring travel.

This position is funded for one year from outside grants and contracts and continuation of the position is subject to the acquisition of additional grant and contract funding.

Responsibilities:

Research, Policy Analysis and Writing

- Handles and conveys detailed and complex criminal justice information determining the most effective format using a variety of methods, such as technical assistance, information requests, and written reports.

- Collects, monitors and summarizes information on legislative action, using a range of research skills, including legal research, surveys and in-depth interviews.

- Analyzes data, interprets and identifies legislative policy implications and trends for our members, including using State Net and other commercial bill and statute databases for research and reporting 50-state policies and actions.

- Writes clearly and concisely for a variety of publications including newsletters, briefing papers, reports, and magazine articles.

- Develops and maintains networks and collaborates with other public interest groups, the private sector, and state, federal or other governmental officials on criminal justice issues.

- Assists as assigned with planning related to NCSL standing committees, Legislative Summit, project meeting events, webinars, or other meetings.

- Assists with current development projects in this and other areas, and identifies new prospects for support.

- Performs other related research, project tasks and responsibilities as assigned.

Police Officer – Metropolitan Police Department, Washington, D.C.

Job source: www.monster.com

About the Job:
The mission of the Metropolitan Police Department is to safeguard the District of Columbia and protect residents and visitors by providing the highest quality of police service with integrity, compassion, and a commitment to innovation that integrates people, technology, and progressive business systems. Discover an organization with a renewed feeling of pride and purpose. We're building a crime-fighting partnership between the police and the community as we develop a new sense of promise and potential within our police department. Help us write a brand new chapter in the history of policing in the District of Columbia.

MPD is a force composed of approximately 3900 sworn officers and 600 civilian employees. To qualify for the position of Police Officer/Experienced Police Officer, you must:

- Be a U.S. citizen at the time of application.

- Be 21 years of age.

- Possess at least 20/100 vision, correctable to 20/30 in both eyes.

- Pass an entry level examination.

- Pass a physical ability test.

- Submit to a polygraph examination.

- Pass a medical examination, including a drug-screening test.

- Pass a psychological examination.

- Possess a high moral character for carrying out law enforcement duties.

- Possess a valid driver's license at the time of application.

Benefits Include:
25 year Retirement – 62.5% of highest three years' salary, upwards to 80% for additional years of service
Family Health and Dental Packages
Paid Family Leave
Overtime and Duty Compensation Pay
Retirement Plan
Accrued Annual & Sick Leave
Tuition Reimbursement Program
Bilingual Pay

- Police Officer (Recruit, Experienced Officer) $55,362 annual

- Cadet $31,820 annual

- Reserve Police Officer – Volunteer

- Intern – Volunteer

- Rental Assistance Program ($1,000 per month for six months, for properties in D.C.)

Requirement(s) Entry-Level Police Officer:

- Successfully completed at least **60 semester hours of college credit** — essentially the equivalent of two years of higher education with course work in any subject matter. Credits from any accredited college or university will be accepted; or

- Served in the Armed Forces of the United States, including the Organized Reserves and National Guard, for **two (2) years on active duty** and, if separated from the military, have received an honorable discharge.

Entry-Level Police candidates must successfully complete our 26 week academy training program.

Corrections, Department of Corrections Unit Supervisor – AODA, Jackson, Wisconsin

Job source: www.linkedin.com

Salary

The starting pay will be between $64,147 and $77,126 per year, plus excellent benefits. Pay on appointment for current state employees may vary according to the applicable pay transaction provisions of the compensation plan and Wisconsin Administrative Code. The pay schedule/range is 81-03. A 12-month probationary period is required.

Assessment Information

51580 - 025 Corrections Unit Supervisor - AODA
Preview Assessment

The Department of Corrections (DOC); Division of Adult Institutions, Jackson Correctional Institution, is recruiting for a Corrections Unit Supervisor - AODA. This position is located in Black River Falls, WI.

Want to make a positive difference in the lives of others? Consider the Wisconsin Department of Corrections. We are focused on public safety through the custody and supervision of offenders. Employees working in the Department of Corrections have the opportunity to positively impact the lives of those in our custody through careers in a variety of fields. DOC uses cutting-edge research and an evidence-based approach to drive service and program delivery, which allows employees to be part of an agency that has a real impact on the people of Wisconsin.

Position Summary

Under the general supervision of the Deputy Warden, the Corrections Unit Supervisor Alcohol and Other Drug Abuse (AODA) position is responsible for the security, general living conditions and activities of all inmates assigned to live and/or participate in programs on the housing unit. This position coordinates multiple discipline areas and provides supervision and direction to assigned unit staff, facilitates and evaluates unit-based work assignments, manages and directs inmate conduct, and manages the daily unit-based services provided to inmates. Included in the major goals of this position are the administration of AODA treatment programs; supervision, direction, and instruction of AODA and Social Work treatment staff for AODA programs; maintaining and updating clinical and administrative procedures; developing appropriate program components; and performing public relations duties.

Special Notes

Applicants must be legally entitled to work in the United States (i.e., a citizen or national of the U.S., a lawful permanent resident, an alien authorized to work in the U.S. without DOC sponsorship) at the time of application. The Department of Corrections will conduct criminal background checks on applicants prior to selection to determine whether the circumstances of any conviction may be related to the job being filled. Upon hire, all new DOC employees are subject to fingerprinting. The Department of Corrections may conduct pre-employment drug screens. Any applicant who is offered employment in a position which requires a pre-employment drug screen must pass the screen as a contingency to employment. Applicants who fail or refuse the drug screen will not be given further consideration for employment.

Qualifications

Special Requirement:

This position includes clinical supervision responsibilities for the institution's AODA program and staff with Substance Abuse Counselor and/or Substance Abuse Counselor in Training.

Therefore, the incumbent must possess or be eligible to possess through the Department of Safety and Professional Services: an Independent Clinical Supervisor license; an Intermediate Clinical Supervisor license; or at a minimum, a Clinical Supervisor in Training license.

Minimally qualified applicants will have experience:

- Program planning and evaluation, coordination and administration (including, but not limited to, specialized support services, treatment programming, etc.)

- Policy and procedure development, implementation, and interpretation (include your specific involvement, e.g., evaluating needs, issue/problem identification, proposing solutions, etc.)

- Leadership or supervision (e.g., assigning/directing/evaluating work, hiring, training, etc.)

Well qualified applicants will have experience:

- Facilitating multi-disciplinary teams or approaches to develop and implement programs

ADVOCACY FOR CRIMINAL JUSTICE: POLICY EXAMPLES

There are only 21 states that oppose the shackling of women who are in labor while they are in prison. The American Medical Association (AMA, 2015) is opposed to the practice of shackling of women who are pregnant and in labor. According to their policy brief:

- Restraining a pregnant woman can pose undue health risks to the woman and her pregnancy.

- Restraining prisoners and detainees increases their potential for physical harm from an accidental trip or fall. The impact of such harm to a pregnant woman can negatively impact her pregnancy.

- Freedom from physical restraints is especially critical during labor, delivery, and postpartum recovery after delivery. Women often need to move around during labor and recovery, including moving their legs as part of the birthing process. Restraints on a pregnant woman can interfere with the medical staff's ability to appropriately assist in childbirth or to conduct sudden emergency procedures.

- Shackling interferes with a mother's ability to care for her baby immediately after delivery and can limit her ability to breast feed.

The AMA proposes the following statewide legislative proposal for states that do not have anti-shackling laws on the books:

(Insert bill number) would require the (insert appropriate prison governing authority) to set uniform standards for how pregnant prisoners are restrained throughout pregnancy, and for implementation of the provisions of (insert bill number.) It will ensure that we maintain safety of correctional workers as well as pregnant prisoners, and will help in enforcement of provisions currently in the Penal Code.

CURYJ (pronounced "courage") in Oakland, CA (https://www.curyj.org/policy-advocacy) targets policies that directly affect youth offenders in prison in California. They have engaged in advocacy at a local level in many innovative ways. One in particular was that they ensured that CURYJ represents 1 of 6 formerly incarcerated people (19 in all) on the Board of State and Community Corrections (BSCC) Prop 47 Executive Steering Committee (ESC). This means their youth representatives are responsible for developing and rating RFPs for 103 million dollars in funding and that formerly incarcerated people played a strong role in crafting the RFPs.

REFERENCES

American Medical Association, Advocacy Resource Center. (2015). *An "Act to prohibit the shackling of pregnant prisoners" model state legislation* (Policy brief). Retrieved from https://www.ama-assn.org/sites/default/files/media-browser/specialty%20group/arc/shackling-pregnant-prisoners-issue-brief.pdf

Boyer, D. (2016, November 30). Obama finalized regulation to "ban the box" on hiring job applicants with criminal records. *Washington Times*. Retrieved from http://www.washingtontimes.com/news/2016/nov/30/obama-finalizes-regulation-ban-box-job-applicants

ADVICE FOR MOVING FORWARD

Maryann Martindale, Senior Policy Advisor, Salt Lake County, Salt Lake City, Utah

When preparing for a career in social justice advocacy, there are many important things to consider.

BACKGROUND AND RÉSUMÉ BUILDING

When planning for a career, involvement in social justice typically begins long before an actual career is established. Those that pursue these careers are already engaged and aware of social issues, have established interest in specific communities or agencies, and have involved themselves in action, typically through volunteer work or other introductory advocacy actions.

Prospective employers look for the candidate with not only a strong education but also a proven track record of actively participating in the issues important to the organization. In anticipation of building a social justice career, it is important to keep a log of all groups, organizations, roles, and other tangible actions taken. These will be the building blocks for a strong social justice résumé that gives added depth and experience to education degrees and certifications.

Your résumé and cover letter are oftentimes the only means you have to communicate with hiring personnel, so think of them as speaking on your behalf.

Oftentimes, job postings will ask for a résumé and an optional cover letter. A cover letter is NEVER optional. Your résumé is your detailed list of qualifications and experience that shows you are competent and appropriately skilled for the job. But your cover letter is your 30-second elevator pitch. This is where you sell yourself.

Your cover letter can convince the hiring personnel reading it that you are passionate about social justice, that you have personal experience working on the issue, and that you are the talented professional that they need for the position. Never underestimate the impact of telling your story—but that story needs to be concise, it needs to be authentic, and it needs to relate directly to the job for which you are applying.

The following pages are examples of a cover letter and résumé.

EXAMPLE COVER LETTER

To Whom It May Concern,

As a new emerging social worker, I am writing you to show my interest in the social work position currently being offered at Henry Mayo Newhall Hospital. I am currently a student at the *insert university name here* and will be graduating this upcoming May 2018. The experience I have gained during my previous internships fits well with the qualifications you are seeking. My second-year internship allowed me to gain experience working with terminally ill patients in a hospital setting while my first-year placement assisted me in gaining experience in working with severe mental illness, substance abuse, and homelessness.

I have worked within a variety of settings with diverse individuals, and this diversity has provided me with many valuable experiences. My career has given me the ability to independently conduct in-depth biopsychosocial assessments and provide help to individuals from various socioeconomic, cultural, ethnic, educational, and other diversified backgrounds. I have conducted pre-transplant psychosocial assessments in both English and Spanish with patients who have end-stage renal disease and require a kidney transplant. I also participated in interdisciplinary team meetings and presented my findings to the transplant team in order to evaluate the transplant candidacy of each patient. I also collaborated and worked closely with health care professionals, such as doctors, nurses, case managers, and clergy. My compassion and empathy toward my patients as well as my bilingual communication skills allow me to easily connect with patients and establish strong rapport.

In addition, my experience has allowed me to provide intensive case management services to those living with severe mental illness, substance abuse, and chronic homelessness. At LA Family Housing, I often administered strengths assessments to assist clients with goal planning and future employment. I participated in the use of crisis intervention and collaborated with the Department of Mental Health to ensure the safety of the client and others through the placing of involuntary psychiatric holds. Wellness checks were also performed routinely to ensure the safety of clients living with a history of trauma, bipolar disorder, schizoaffective disorder, and illegal drug and alcohol use.

In addition to my clinical skills, I have many personal skills that support my knowledge and sensitivity. I offer commitment, excitement, organization, passion, and professionalism: qualities that are necessary for providing leadership and promoting a positive work environment and client relationship.

After you have reviewed my résumé, I would be delighted to meet you in person to further discuss the possibility of joining your organization.

Thank you for your time,
Insert name here

EXAMPLE RÉSUMÉ

NAME
Address
E-mail
Phone number

California State University Channel Islands   Camarillo, CA
Bachelor of Arts, Psychology   May 2015

TRAININGS
60-hour certification class to become a sexual assault advocate 2013

SKILLS
Languages: Fluent in Spanish
Computer: Proficient in Microsoft Office, PowerPoint

EXPERIENCE

Valley Trauma Center, Van Nuys, CA   2013–2014
Sexual Assault Advocate

- Answered crisis hotline calls regarding sexual assault, domestic violence, and suicidality in an effort to assist community members and direct them to internal or external services.

- Accompanied survivors of rape and sexual assault to forensic examinations at the Center for Assault Treatment Services (CATS).

- Provided crisis intervention and support services in order to empower survivors of rape and sexual assault in making their own decisions about whether or not to file charges with the local police department.

- Created safe environment for callers over the phone so that they could share their stories and receive the help they needed.

- Advocated for clients to make sure that they received the physical health and mental health treatment they desired.

(Continued)

(Continued)

Ruslana Kadze, MD, Tarzana, CA   2013–2014
Shadowing at Physician's Office and Providence Tarzana Hospital

- Helped provide compassionate support for patients during painful procedures in labor and delivery.

- Eased pregnant patient's concerns by measuring fetal heart rate with a Doppler.

- Documented patient history in each chart and educated each patient in understanding the process and risks of their surgical procedures.

Providence Tarzana Medical Center, Tarzana, CA   2011–2012
Nursing Station Volunteer

- Exposed to hospital environment and assisted patients in navigating the hospital system.

Firetect Flame Retardants, Canyon Country, CA   2008–2009
Administrative Office Assistant

- Worked with customers who came into the office by answering questions and following up on their orders for flame retardants.

- Accounting experience using QuickBooks system entering bills and deposits.

- Prepared invoices to be billed to the customers.

- Scheduled shipping in a timely manner for customer products and followed up on deliveries.

GETTING THE INTERVIEW

If you are invited to interview, you've passed the first test. In the job market today, it is not unusual for hiring managers to receive hundreds of résumés for a single position. Once you've cleared that first hurdle, your skills at interviewing will determine whether or not you continue in the hiring process as a candidate.

Learn about the company. Read their website, speak to people you may know about their work, know who the principals are, and understand the organization's mission. Ideally, you will have done some of this preliminary work prior to applying, but you need to do a thorough review before an interview.

Job interviews take us out of our comfort zone and require us to not only show our confidence in our work but to articulate that confidence. It can be a tough transition, and not all great candidates are great self-promoters. Practice with a friend. Try out your pitch on someone you trust to give you honest feedback. Practice your questions in a mirror. The more comfortable you are selling yourself, the more authentic it will be when you put it into use.

We've all heard the advice, "Dress for the job you want, not the one you have." This applies to interviewing as well. If it is a casual environment, it is not necessary to wear a suit, but keep in mind, you should never be the most casual person in the room. An interviewer will expect an applicant to show a sense of personal pride and to be professional. Wait until after you've gotten the job to join in on casual Friday. Make no mistake, they're judging what you wear, not just your résumé.

THE INTERVIEW

Interviews are daunting. It doesn't matter how prepared you are or how comfortable you are with your skills, what you say and do dictates whether or not you move on in the hiring process. It is stressful. Understanding and accepting that from the outset can help you be better prepared.

The purpose of an interview is for you to articulate why you are the best candidate for the job. They will judge not only your skills, but how you articulate them; you need to express your passion for their issue and mission. Be prepared with questions. This is not as difficult as it sounds, especially if you're knowledgeable about the company. Be thoughtful in your questions. Think about these well in advance of the interview and take notes as you are preparing yourself.

Be prepared with specific examples of things you have done that support the mission of the company or show that you are skilled to do so.

It is okay to take notes during an interview; in fact, it will show you are truly interested and not just giving them a canned speech. Ask the hiring manager or human resources (HR) contact for the correct name, spelling, and contact e-mail for anyone you meet and use this after the interview for your follow-up thank-you e-mails.

NOW WHAT?

You created a solid résumé, you were prepared for your interview, and you believe it went well. Now comes what can be the most frustrating part of the job hunt—waiting. Once an organization has started the interview process, it can still take several weeks for them to come to a decision. There are a few things you will be tempted to do but should not.

The first of these is aggressive follow-up. After every interview, you should send a follow-up thank-you e-mail. Although it is a good idea to check back in if you haven't heard back after a week, do not hound the hiring manager or person with whom you interviewed. You want to be memorable but for the right reasons—your ability to fill the job, not your ability to annoy them the most.

Second, do not stop your job search. You may believe that you were the perfect fit for your perfect job, but there are myriad things that go into hiring someone and you may not check off the right boxes, from their perspective. When you put all your energy into a single position, and you are not offered the job, it can be a real hit to your confidence. It is important to keep looking, keep interviewing, and keep a positive outlook.

Third, DO NOT, under any circumstances, lie to them about your job prospects. It may be tempting to tell them you have another offer to try and get them to move. But if you're one of their finalists and they aren't certain yet, you may just give them the opening to choose another candidate. Your timing does not dictate theirs. Stay focused on your broader job search while keeping in regular but not constant contact with those you've met.

Most importantly, stay positive. The dedication and commitment it takes to pursue a career in social justice advocacy will be evident in your skills, résumé, and your passion, and being patient will reward you with the right career fit.

FINAL WORDS FROM THE AUTHOR

I have about a thousand inspirational quotes all around my office that keep me going. They are about taking risk, approaching my work from a space of love, and letting the light I have in me shine in the lives of others.

In the past 5 years I have turned to social media (particularly Twitter) to build a community of social workers and social justice advocates who do the work around the world that I am interested in. I have connected with people whom I never would have met otherwise, and they have enriched my life and my capacity to engage in badass social justice advocacy no matter where I am.

I want to leave you with some inspiration from social justice workers from all over the nation who responded to this question on Facebook and Twitter, "I am writing a book on careers in social justice advocacy. What is one piece of advice you would give someone who wants to engage in social justice work?" I received many responses, which I will summarize here:

- You have to find your own voice; authenticity is key to advocacy.

- Be kind to yourself so that the work can be done.

- Patience and fortitude are key because our systems are remarkably broken.

- This is not a short-term career; you have to be in it for the long haul because there is always something to do.

- Taking the long view and realizing it isn't about you is critical to a successful career.

- Many times you will be seen as the opposition and not the ally, so persistence is critical to success.

- You can't make change if you don't put yourself out there.

- Don't take yourself or your work too seriously, and always have one person in your life who can tell you when you screw up so you can always improve.

- Social justice advocacy has to take place in the workplace, too.

- You don't have to be good at everything to know you are contributing to change.

- Follow your passion because if you truly believe in the work you are doing, you will be able to keep your internal fire alight.